Jean-Luc Nancy
and Christian Thought

Jean-Luc Nancy and Christian Thought

Deconstructions of the Bodies of Christ

Christina Smerick

LEXINGTON BOOKS
Lanham • Boulder • New York • London

Published by Lexington Books
An imprint of The Rowman & Littlefield Publishing Group, Inc.
4501 Forbes Boulevard, Suite 200, Lanham, Maryland 20706
www.rowman.com

Unit A, Whitacre Mews, 26-34 Stannary Street, London SE11 4AB

Copyright © 2018 by Lexington Books

All rights reserved. No part of this book may be reproduced in any form or by any electronic or mechanical means, including information storage and retrieval systems, without written permission from the publisher, except by a reviewer who may quote passages in a review.

British Library Cataloguing in Publication Information Available

Library of Congress Cataloging-in-Publication Data Available

Library of Congress Control Number: 2017955869

ISBN 978-1-4985-2156-7 (clothr)
ISBN 978-1-4985-2157-4 (electronic)
ISBN 978-1-4985-2158-1 (pbk.)

Contents

Acknowledgments	vii
The Bodies of Christ	ix
1 Thinking the Incarnation	1
2 Raising Up the Body of Christ	27
3 Eucharist, Prayer, Faith: The Body of Christ-the-Church	57
Why Christianity?	91
Bibliography	97
Index	101
About the Author	105

Acknowledgments

I would like to express my gratitude to everyone who put up with me as I labored at this work, particularly Brian Hartley, Ben Wayman, Lori Gaffner, and Ruth Huston at Greenville University. In particular, I want to thank John Brittingham, Eric Severson, and Paul Stroble for their encouragement and for the comments and suggestions they provided me. Many thanks as well to Greenville University for the sabbatical leave that allowed me to finish this book. Finally, many thanks to Ryan, Mackenzie, and Sylvie, who put up with many rambling conversations at the dinner table as I compulsively shared interesting tidbits about obscure church fathers; and to my father, Peter Smerick, without whose constant encouragement I would not be in academics at all.

The Bodies of Christ

Jacques Derrida has said, "Only Christianity can do this work, that is, undo it while doing it.... Dechristianization will be a Christian victory."[1] Jean-Luc Nancy asks, "Why Christianity?"[2] Or, more specifically, why Christianity *still*, why Christianity *now*? Why are we still talking about Christianity? Any secular thinker can be forgiven for feeling exasperated, even exhausted, that in spite of scientific and industrial revolutions, the rise of modernity, the development of technologies and economies on a global scale, we are still talking about a religion originating in the backwater of the Roman Empire, started by a group of peasants, which had achieved world domination largely due to political luck. Yet Christianity lingers; it lurks in unlikely places, it haunts our politics and our metaphysics. And it does more than haunt and lurk like a lost specter—it also carries with it the spell of its own unraveling, its own deconstruction.

Jean-Luc Nancy's works span decades and range widely in subject and tone, moving from aesthetics to ontology to community to freedom, and finding elements ripe for deconstruction in everything from paintings of the Resurrection to his own heart transplant. Yet what has increasingly haunted his writings from 1995 forward has been the sneaking suspicion that the growing catastrophe of the world, the "unworlding" of the world, finds both its origin and perhaps its solution in the deconstruction of its dominant religion: Christianity. Even as Nancy asks, with some exasperation, "why Christianity?" he cannot leave it alone—for it will not leave us alone.[3]

Nancy's work, philosophically speaking, can be understood as a critical, yet productive, response to both Martin Heidegger and Friedrich Nietzsche. Adopting both thinkers' eviscerations of Western metaphysics and onto-theology, Nancy's earlier writings primarily commented upon other, earlier philosophers, but particularly after his heart transplant in the early 1990s, he begins—in the midst of pain and numerous health issues—to come into his own, producing significant works particularly on notions of community or "being-with."[4] We find his earliest explorations into religion as well, notably in *The Inoperative Community*. Significant works on globalization and aesthetics from both a political and philosophical perspective follow, as well as an ever-deepening engagement with the body and embodiment.[5]

Nancy's works on monotheism and Christianity, broadly speaking, tackle Western monotheisms' intersections with art and aesthetics, politics, the body, and creation itself. In this, his work follows conversations in French sociology regarding secularization: whether religions are dying out as influencers and shapers of culture, or whether their roles have been usurped by science, popular culture, and/or the state, while retaining a theological mission (that of world dominance). The debate between Karl Löwith and Hans Blumenberg regarding how to define the term "secularization" shaped subsequent thinkers, such as Marcel Gauchet, who claimed that Christianity may be the Western religion *par excellence,* in that it is a "religion for the departure from religion."[6]

In other words, Christianity itself has an integral role in the secularization of the Western world.[7] As Jean-Claude Monod writes regarding the Western mission to civilize the world, "This view of a historical mission is, according to Löwith, *unthinkable without and inseparable from* the Christian past of the West."[8] Nancy picks up this conversation, claiming that Blumenberg "failed to answer" the question regarding secularization, and thus Nancy pursues, in his own way, how "the whole of our thought is Christian through and through…"[9] Nancy is shaped and informed by this question raised (and not answered) by Löwith and Blumenberg: Are we really experiencing a "de-theologization" of the world, or rather are we witnessing the role of religion being played by other actors? And can we claim that we are freed from the religious past of the West in either case?

The issue with Western monotheism, and Christianity in particular, is that in establishing an ontology grounded or founded upon one god, one horizon or limit, monotheism makes the world one, flattening or denying its multiplicities and pluralities. This is reflected in the process of economic and political globalization, and it brings forth an understanding of the world and those in it that categorizes and politicizes us to death, encompassing the globe, destroying difference.[10] The modern secular age has kept its universal task of world salvation, emptied of its otherworldly trappings. Uncovering the roots of this universal task in the religions we have supposedly left behind may enable us to free ourselves from this so-called salvation.

In *The Creation of the World* and "Of Divine Places" (in *The Inoperative Community*), Nancy examines the roots of monotheism via the creation myth. The monotheistic creation story sets up a dichotomous structure that presumes a oneness to humanity emerging from the singularity of an external

Creator. Nancy pushes back against this myth by eviscerating the fantasy of a singular Being beyond this world, and instead draws our attention to how human beings, together yet diverse, make the world as it is, in spite of the prevailing mythos. The goal of Western monotheism—to make one the world—is a self-contradictory goal, in that it destroys what actually makes the world: difference, plurality, the space between you and me that lets us work together. Yet monotheism sows the seeds of its own destruction by making God singular and outside, not immanent: monotheism becomes an a-theism, as God is no longer present in the world but exists outside of it. The hollowing out of the place of God re-introduces space in our world—spaces to breathe and be together without being one and the same. This is the absenting of God, an absence that pervades all of Nancy's work on religion. God, in being understood as other than the world and outside it, is not immanent or present. Monotheism worships an absent God.

This self-deconstruction of monotheism finds its best, most ironic un-working in Western Christianity. As Nancy writes in *The Inoperative Community,* a "man-god" is the "totally secular divinity of humanity," the making divine of the individual human, complicating the absence of an external Being by introducing a present, then absent, man-god about whom we must construct meanings and elaborate theologies.[11] Thus, while Christianity and Western Christian doctrine (aka the documents, creeds, and councils established by the early church prior to 1064CE) cover a wide range of topics, the one figure or trope Nancy engages with primarily is that of Christ himself, the man-god.

Nancy's works on Christ emerge from this examination of monotheism in general to a more focused account of Christianity, found primarily in the *Dis-Enclosure* volumes and in *Noli Me Tangere*. One also finds the body of Christ as the focus in sections of *Corpus*. Quite a few philosophers have provided excellent accounts of this trajectory of Nancy's work on Christianity: Ian James and Daniele Rugo, in particular.[12] In every case, I find myself in general agreement with their claims: Nancy draws his motifs and tropes from a non-mystical, all-too-human Christianity, a Christianity devoid of God. Indeed, the body of Christ in Nancy's reading is a body *absent* of God, a singular body, yet multiplied in Christianity: body as wounded, as opened, as dead, as resurrected and glorified, and as consumed. This body sets forth a possibility for thought that leads us to a (not-yet) ontology of the body, of the present that is bereft of Presence, and of a world outside of which there is truly nothing.

This complex and contradictory wrestling with the body of Christ, however, fails to show up in much of Christian practice, in the thinking and living of many Christians. To suggest that this a/theologized body is *Christian* would be considered scandalous to many faithful Christians; but to *deny* that this is Christian may be blasphemous. The scandal of an absent, or worse, non-existent God would outrage the average Christian; yet, the very construction of the person of Jesus via the doctrines and debates of the early Church require the average Christian to admit that God is acknowledged as absent by Christ himself.[13] Christianity, the thinking of Christianity, carries this absented *body* with it, yet this thinking is at odds with much of what we see those *practicing* the Christian religion doing, claiming, and seeking. Christian dogma carries with it an empty tomb and a paradoxical God-man; all too often, Christian practice (or lived Christian faith) often participates in more of what Nancy would call the globalization of the world: a universalizing morality, a belief in the oneness of humanity and thus the need for one kind of salvation. Christianity carries with it an absent God—a God who may be "with us," but who also ascended bodily and who perhaps even abandoned that body as it hung on the cross. Christian practice, however, can tend to avoid thinking that abandonment in favor of worshiping an ever-present invisible spirit-God. The openness or absence gapes in every creed: Christian doctrine claims that Jesus' flesh is divine, but his flesh is/was abandoned; his flesh is now also risen, abandoning us, becoming absent.[14] The body in Christian *practice*—in the monotheism Nancy warns us about—is codified, (de)sexualized, and moralized. The *body* of God, the distinctive of Christianity, hanging on crosses in Catholic and Orthodox churches and dwelling in hearts throughout Protestantism, is *absent* in the sense that it is simply not thought about. Therefore, while I read Nancy in similar ways to my philosophical brethren, I also take this deconstruction as critique of Christian practice, beyond what Nancy would wish.

Nancy makes it clear that he is not advocating a return to religion, or even a turn, and he seeks "an expansion of the atheist world."[15] Yet, almost immediately after making this bold, clear statement, he returns to the notion that Christianity, in some strange way, manages to free the history of the West from its own prison, even as Christianity was part of that incarceration. Western history has moved from a sense of the world that is self-contained and without discontinuity to a world of tragedy where all life is insignificant, to this brave new world (view) in which "the sense of the world opens as a spacing"—firstly, of course, as a sense of a world outside/above this world, but then, as that heaven moves farther away from the imagination, and a looming, gaping nothing remains, this brave new world elicits a reason that is "opened up," a thinking that "dis-encloses" as Christianity deconstructs itself with its own meanings and languages.[16]

For Nancy, then, there is no Being who is Other, outside the world, creating, informing, judging, etc., but rather there is "space-that-is-not-me-or-us." What is other to us is not an Other, but our very be-ing-as-doing, our language, our actions. I agree with Jason Alvis, who argues that, while Nancy is not aligned with the theological turn taken in phenomenology and vociferously criticized by Dominique Janicaud, he is not turning against religion in the manner accorded modernity and scientific discourse.[17] Nor is Nancy suggesting that phenomenology and theology become one, or address the same thing. Rather, as Alvis puts it,

> A phenomenology of the inapparent [which he claims Nancy is exploring via Heidegger] [i]s that which threatens the disciplinary optimism of both theology and phenomenology.... He is not interested in policing the territory between the supposed dichotomies of philosophy (and its immanent phenomena) and theology (which is beholden to an invisible transcendence), but to find means of provocation of the limits of both disciplines in order to make us more human.[18]

Nancy's exposure of the deconstruction of Christianity is performed not to bring Christianity back from the brink or correct it, but rather to reveal its kenotic heart.[19]

What I find most fascinating in his wide-ranging writings on the subject is the motif of the body of Christ itself in its multiplicities. While, as I have said, there are any number of doctrines and theological arguments one could extrapolate and explore via Nancy's writings, his concomitant interest in both Christianity and the body have drawn me to Christ himself and the doctrines, beliefs, and constructions pertaining specifically to the ways the historical church has used the phrase "body of Christ." The person of Jesus Christ is an obvious motif upon which to focus, of course, but more pertinently, the body of Christ provides a dual theme to trace throughout Nancy's own corpus, organizing a rather disparate set of texts.

Nancy's thought is often like a lightning strike, illuminating an unanticipated opening. Nevertheless, if his work has a flaw, it is that it all too often seems to begin in the middle. Particularly in his essays on Christianity, much is assumed regarding the reader's knowledge of Christian doctrine, Origen, Irenaeus, Tertullian, etc. Nancy himself points out that many who are impatient to get on with the death of God already are skipping a fundamental, necessary practice, that of engaging Christianity in the first place. Nevertheless, his own scans on Christianity are difficult to follow, and difficult to trust, if one does not have any grounding in that to which he is responding.

When we turn to the secondary literature on Nancy, we find little help. Those outside of philosophical circles concerned with hermeneutics, phenomenology, and deconstruction do not seem to have engaged Nancy's works on Christianity as much. His writings on globalization and ontology, on art and touching, have been consumed, responded to, unpacked, and elaborated upon by significant philosophers (most notably, of course, his friend Jacques Derrida), such that one may find a rich and rewarding bibliography of secondary works on these topics. But most of these have spent rather less time on his work on Christianity itself (a notable exception is the work of various philosophers in *Re-Treating Religion: Deconstructing Christianity with Jean-Luc Nancy* and Gregg Lambert's *Return Statements*). Some thinkers are entirely sympathetic with Nancy's desire to save the world from religion; others are more concerned with how his work on Christianity relates and expands upon his work on globalization, ontology, and capital.[20] However, in all but a few cases, the writers in question—as far as I can tell—hold to no faith of their own, and are not intimately familiar with the doctrines or theological history of the Western church.[21] All are philosophers in terms of training, so it is no surprise that they are not patristics experts. What is lacking is a thorough-going *engagement with* Nancy's exploration of Christianity's auto-deconstruction, using the *resources* of Christianity.[22]

I, too, am a philosopher by training and no expert in patristics. Nevertheless, as I have written elsewhere, I find myself living and writing at a boundary, a line or division between my discipline and my faith (a decidedly awkward Christianity).[23] As such, I found myself longing for someone to make the connections, to trace back the sources of Nancy's deconstruction to the documents, teachings, and dogmas of the Church itself as they pertain to the body of Christ. As I did not find what I sought, I have here tried to create it—and to create, as well, a bridge between Nancy's work and the work of postmodern theologians, writing in and from marginal spaces themselves. As Nancy repurposes Christological and theological language in order to achieve, in an incomplete sense, a world without Other, without transcendence, a world that gives itself to itself from within itself as openings, spacings, so I try to find the spaces within Christianity—specifically within the various bodies of Christ envisioned, imagined, and extrapolated from Christian doctrine and practice—in which the very doctrines coming to an end provide the seeds for self-deconstruction.

Thus, the trajectory of this book is to orient Nancy's interpretations of the body of Christ in the Incarnation, the Resurrection, and the practices of the Church to the dogmas from which they arise and in which they have their complex articulations. In each case, I first explore Nancy's undoing, deconstructing, and reinventing of Christian motifs regarding the body (bodies) of Christ, and then explore the various Christian traditions with regard to the topic at hand. Additionally, I strive to place Nancy in conversation with current theologians in order to demonstrate that the deconstruction of Christianity is indeed ongoing, and coming from within the guild, the Church, and the seminary, not just from without. Indeed, I will claim that it is only from within that a deconstruction of the kind Nancy hopes for can take place.

Chapter 1: Thinking the Incarnation of Christ provides a reading of Nancy's work on the body alongside his ongoing deconstructing of Christianity to give us a glimpse of how the body of Christ in or as incarnation works as a preface to an ontology of the body, which according to Nancy has yet-to-be-thought. In God-becoming-man, God disappears from sight, a man is glorified and anointed, and the world is exposed to itself—not to an outside space, not to something that is Other, but to the Other that is itself.[24] This understanding or thinking of the body is prefigured in Christian dogma regarding the body of God. After exposing the various ways Nancy takes up the body of the incarnation, I turn to the early Church Fathers (patristics) and the foundational creeds in order to demonstrate where and how the body of Christ in or as the incarnation undoes philosophical theology. I also examine kenosis theology, which provides an understanding of the incarnation closest (although still far) to Nancy's own more positive account. Finally, I find echoes of his thinking in post-modern theology, notably the works of Cheri DiNovo and Craig Keen. DiNovo performs queer theology, reading Christianity against the grain to uncover its destabilizing weirdness. Keen resists categorization, but operates as a post-ontological systematic theologian: he consistently focuses on untangling theology from onto-theology. Both DiNovo and Keen provide us with alternative deconstructions of the incarnation, from within the guild of theology, very broadly construed.

Chapter 2: Raising Up the Body of Christ addresses the resurrection narratives in Scripture, and the ways Nancy has extrapolated them into a immanent image of Death, rather than into a new, embodied life. Nancy addresses the concept of the resurrection briefly in *The Inoperative Community,* and more substantially in *Noli Me Tangere, Dis-Enclosure,* and in various interviews. In almost every case, he reinterprets resurrection quite tangentially to orthodox Christian interpretations. Whereas in orthodox Christianity, Christ's resurrection is the site of hope and salvation, the confirmation of God's promise, and the conquering of death, Nancy interprets Christ's resurrection as death continued rather than overcome.[25] Likewise, in *Noli Me Tangere*, Nancy argues that resurrection is not death vanquished, but death "extended indefinitely."[26] Examining the metaphors and theories that drive the early Church's faith in resurrection, we do not find a singular, absolute doctrine, but rather a complex array of images, along with multiple resurrections (Lazarus, Jesus, the general resurrection). As such, it is not a stretch to see how Christianity here provides ongoing re-interpretations of this faith claim. The chapter ends by tracing treatments of the resurrection in the theology of Karl Barth, and the feminist theological work of Andrea Bieler and Luise Schottroff, who examine the Eucharist through the lens of resurrection, inviting an embodied experience of Christ. Craig Keen's work is helpful again as well—his insistence that the body of Christ resurrected remains a mutilated body has tremendous significance when paired with Nancy's writings regarding wounds. Finally, the work of Brian Robinette in *Grammars of Resurrection* demonstrates how a theologian of a phenomenological persuasion may engage in unpacking Christian doctrine, multiplying it and fragmenting its worldly political powers, without abandoning faith altogether.

The final chapter, *Eucharist, Prayer, Faith: The Body of Christ-the-Church,* examines the body of Christ as the Church, a motif established through the words of Christ to Peter and expanded upon in Paul's letters. This chapter is structured somewhat differently, given the tripartite themes that run through it. I begin with the Eucharist, first exploring Nancy's references to it, examining the early Church writings regarding its function, purpose, and ethical import. Then, returning to post-modern theology—notably to Bieler and Schottroff and to Susan A. Ross—I present current interpretations that push against the patriarchal dominance of the altar and the ritual. Again, I briefly examine Keen's work before turning to William T. Cavanaugh's exemplary work, *Torture and Eucharist*. After exploring the various ways of interpreting the consumed body of Christ as Eucharist, I turn to the church itself as the body of Christ, examining the activities of prayer or adoration as the workings of the body of Christ-the-Church by diving into Nancy's latest work on Christianity, *Adoration: The Deconstruction of Christianity II*. In this work, Nancy rescues prayer from religion, recovering its ethical, active dimension and its sense of address, but directing that *salut* not to a heaven above, but linguistically to this strange world of sense, to these beings with us, to the "real" of the world as it is. I call this a recovery because a quick examination of the early Church, particularly of the Desert Fathers, reveals this notion of prayer as called or elicited, as active, and as ethical—as acts of love and mercy rather than an interiorized monologue with oneself. In modern theology as well, there is a re-turn toward prayer as corporate, rather than individualistic, and as *work* rather than as mere mental correspondence. The work of Lawrence Paul Hemming, a Catholic theologian, is particularly helpful here.

Finally, I turn to faith, the subject of a number of essays by Nancy and something at the heart of his call for justice. In Nancy's "A Faith That Is Nothing at All," drawing from the letter of James, faith is precipitated by, yes, nothing at all, and only shows up in *action*, not in mental assent to a proposition or to a certainty (as "belief" does, in Nancy's estimate). I once more turn to the early Church Fathers to demonstrate that they also distinguish between faith and belief, and, in the final analysis, insist upon a life *lived in faith*, rather than simple mental certainties carried forward by an otherwise unchanged person. Finally, I come full circle back to the work of Cheri DiNovo in *Que(e)rying Evangelism*, reflecting upon how this looks in practice, in a Western North American church that is trying to work out its faith with fear and trembling, rather than with ecclesial backing and power games. I end, as seems fitting, with the theologian whose work most echoes Nancy's own: Craig Keen.

Just as the paintings Nancy analyzes in *Noli Me Tangere* were not created to allow for a deconstruction of resurrection, I recognize that Nancy's work is not designed nor intended to help support or buttress claims made in Christian doctrine or theology. Nevertheless, I intend to do that work not in order to reify doctrine or prop up a kind of onto-theology or theology of transcendence, both of which well deserve the critique that Nancy and others provide, but rather, to hold a mirror to Christian theology itself in order to reveal the very things that Nancy himself discovers in Christian doctrine: the deconstructive tendencies. But I do so using the very doctrines that Nancy draws from. Just as Nancy himself uses Christian doctrines in order to trace a deconstruction where Christianity undoes itself, I am using Nancy's account of said doctrines not to work against deconstruction or to work against Nancy, but rather to play out or trace back the origins of these ideas, such that perhaps Christianity can indeed complete the work it begins in its deconstructive tendencies. I am audacious enough to suggest that this may be the mission of the Church in the first place, a mission covered over by centuries of becoming powers and principalities rather than servants and martyrs.

NOTES

1. Jacques Derrida. *On Touching.*
2. Jean-Luc Nancy, *The Inoperative Community*, ed. Peter Connor, trans. Peter Connor et al (Minneapolis, MN: University of Minnesota Press, 1991), 138.
3. It may be helpful to clarify that much of what I reference in the introduction is more akin to Søren Kierkegaard's "Christendom" than to the religious practice of Christianity as a diverse religion comprised of multiple bodies.
4. See Jean-Luc Nancy, *Being Singular Plural*, trans. Robert Richardson and Anne O'Byrne (Redwood City, CA: Stanford University Press, 2000).
5. See Jean-Luc Nancy, *The Birth to Presence*, trans. Brian Holmes et al (Redwood City, CA: Stanford University Press, 1993); *The Sense of the World*, trans. Jeffrey Librett (Minneapolis, MN: University of Minnesota Press, 1997) and *The Experience of Freedom*, trans. Bridget McDonald (Redwood City, CA: Stanford University Press, 1994). For his work on embodiment, see *Corpus*, trans. Richard A. Rand (New York, NY: Fordham University Press, 2008).
6. Marcel Gauchet, *The Disenchantment of the World: A Political History of Religion*, trans. Oscar Burge (Princeton, NJ: Princeton University Press, 1997), 4.
7. This is reflected, in part, in Gianni Vattimo's argument regarding Christianity as "weak thought," and as the sower of the seeds of secularization, in his *After Christianity*, trans. Luca D'Isanto (New York: Columbia University Press, 2002). Vattimo tends to focus primarily on Christianity's immanence, rather than transcendence.
8. Jean-Claude Monod, "Heaven on Earth? The Löwith-Blumenberg Debate," *Radical Secularization?* Ed. Stijn Latre et al. (New York: Bloomsbury Publishing, 2015).
9. Jean-Luc Nancy, *Dis-Enclosure: The Deconstruction of Christianity*, trans. Bettina Bergo et al. (New York: Fordham Press, 2008) 9, 142.
10. This view of monotheistic religion as a generally held belief in a world beyond or outside of this one owes much to the various proponents of the "secularization thesis" (really, theses) in sociology. In particular, Marcel Gauchet argued that this is what religion is: a belief in a world outside of ours, a subjective conviction; secularization, then, is the loss of this belief or "worldview." Gauchet refers to this as a "disenchantment," which carries with it a sense of loss. The enchantment was, at one time, "common sense"—a view or understanding of the world that most people hold and that shapes society. Disenchantment is that subjective loss of sense-making—a topic Nancy spends most of his writings working out. See Philip S. Gorski and Ates Altınordu's brief overview in "After Secularization?" *Annual Review of Sociology.* 34 (2008) and Andre Cloots, "Christianity, Incarnation, and Disenchantment," *Radical Secularization?*, 2015.
11. Jean-Luc Nancy, *The Inoperative Community*, 139.

12. Ian James, *The Fragmentary Demand: An Introduction to the Philosophy of Jean-Luc Nancy* (Redwood City, CA: Stanford University Press, 2005). Daniele Rugo, *Jean-Luc Nancy and the Thinking of Otherness: Philosophy and Powers of Existence* (London, UK: Bloomsbury Press, 2013).

13. Jesus cries out on the cross, "My God, why have you forsaken me?" (Matthew 27:46).

14. See above endnote—yet Jesus' body is also seen as transfigured and holy: "and they took hold of his feet, and worshiped him" (Matthew 28:9). Likewise, Jesus bodily ascends into heaven (Luke 24:51). See also the debate between Nestorius and Cyril of Alexandria on the two natures of Christ and their relationship to the body of Christ. The Christian Church ended up siding with Cyril, claiming that Mary did indeed give birth to not only the physical body of Christ and his human nature, but to his divine nature as well. The two natures of Christ form one person (*prosopon*).

15. Jean-Luc Nancy, *Adoration*, trans. John McKeane (New York: Fordham University Press, 2013), 22.

16. Ibid., 24.

17. See Dominique Janicaud, "The Theological Turn of French Phenomenology," *Phenomenology and the "Theological Turn": The French Debate*, trans. Bernard G. Prusak (New York: Fordham University Press, 2000), 16-106.

18. Jason Alvis, "Holy Phenomenology: Heidegger's 'Phenomenology of the Inapparent' in Jean-Luc Nancy's *Adoration: The Deconstruction of Christianity II*," *Literature & Theology 29: 4* (2015), 442-3.

19. From *kenosis*: the self-renunciation of God in Christ, taken primarily from Paul's letter to the Philippians, 2:7: "…but *emptied himself*, taking the form of a slave…"

20. For example, Christopher Watkin's work on Nancy, Badiou, and Meillassoux is masterful, but focuses primarily on how each thinker fails to escape theism: "in deconstructing Christianity Nancy imitates Christianity, or at least cannot conclusively be said not to imitate Christianity," *Difficult Atheism: Post-Theological Thinking in Alain Badiou, Jean-Luc Nancy and Quentin Meillassoux* (Edinburgh, UK: Edinburgh University Press, 2011), 39. He does note, however, that Nancy seems to head beyond or behind Christianity into a deconstruction of the "a/theism binary per se" but that he ultimately fails to "escape the shadow of the theological" (41, 111). Mark Lewis Taylor engages Nancy in his *The Theological and the Political: On the Weight of the World*, as well. Taylor is a theologian who is against transcendence, and against the "guild" of theology. He utilizes Foucault and Nancy in their analyses of power to unpack how theology could operate in this world without transcendence, but does not engage explicitly much of Nancy's work on Christianity itself.

21. One exception to this trend is the work of Peter Joseph Fritz, who has engaged Nancy's work from an orthodox Catholic perspective in several key articles. However, his focus is so narrowly upon what Nancy could have to say to the Roman Catholic Church, particularly regarding Mary, that I found it to be fairly inapplicable to my broader questions. Likewise, his work on Nancy, Christianity, and capitalism, seems to make a straw man of one of Nancy's asides (linking Christianity unambiguously to capitalism). See bibliography for article information.

22. François Raffoul uses this word "resources" to indicate the history of ideas and practices that comprise the complex and sometimes contradictory documents of the Western Christian tradition.

23. See "Bodies, Communities, Faith: Christian Legacies in Jean-Luc Nancy," in *Analecta Hermeneutica*. No. 4 (2012).

24. Again, Nancy is not the first philosopher, nor even the first French philosopher, to have explored the ambiguities of the incarnation. Andre Cloots, in an essay on Gauchet, summarizes well the "fragile" history of the incarnation:

> The doctrine of Incarnation in its final form was the result of fierce theological battles during the first centuries of the Christian era…. All these battles were related to the interpretation of Incarnation, and thus of the relation between heaven and earth, between the divinity and the humanity of Jesus, between God and man,

between transcendence and immanence, and eventually between the rejection or the acceptance of the world.

Cloots, "Christianity, Incarnation and Disenchantment," 52.

25. By "orthodox" Christianity, I mean not Orthodox Christianity but the set of creeds accepted by the vast majority of denominations and churches who call themselves Christian. There will always be some outliers.

26. Jean-Luc Nancy, *Noli Me Tangere: On the Raising of the Body*, trans. Sarah Clift et al (New York: Fordham University Press, 2008), 17.

Chapter One

Thinking the Incarnation

> We believe in one God, the Father almighty, maker of heaven and earth, of all things visible and invisible. And in one Lord Jesus Christ, the only Son of God, begotten from the Father before all ages . . . begotten, not made; of the same essence as the Father.
>
> —Nicene Creed, 325 C.E.

Belief in the incarnation of God in the person of Jesus of Nazareth is one of the main tenets of the Christian faith. It is also one of the more bizarre developments in the history of Western religions. While parallels can and have been drawn between the incarnation and the deification of emperors, the demi-gods of Rome and Greece, and the many manifestations of Krishna, the incarnation of God in Jesus cannot, at the end, be equated easily or simply with any of these other boundary-crossings between deity and humanity. Monotheism makes this incarnation much more complex and paradoxical.

The incarnation of God in Christ opens the way for thousands of years of philosophical and theological gymnastics, and it opens the way as well for Christianity's own deconstruction, using its own terms. Without the incarnation, Christianity collapses into an apocalyptic Judaism or neo-Platonism. The im/possibility of the eternal God becoming a singular human being lies at the heart of Christianity, and initiates an uneasy joining of incommensurates, one that remains an irritant in its systems even, or especially, now.

Rather than an enemy that must be combatted, Christian thought can be an (unwitting at times) ally to the project of deconstructing Western hegemony and exploding the massive monism that Western monotheism and philosophy have helped produce. Nancy himself gives voice to this in his seminal essay, "The Deconstruction of Christianity." He writes, "It is…in the disassembling of the philosophical constituents of Christian dogma or Christian theology that we must perceive the philosophemes of the proclamation" which Christianity essentially is.[1] We must examine not only the proclamations in Scripture, but their dogmatic development, finding therein the "infinite opening of the sense" of being that undermines the philosophical systems theology has often sought to uphold. Rather than a closed, self-referential system that defines meaning, Christian doctrine can instead, in spite of itself, provide openings for meaning-generation that are multiple rather than singular, and playful rather than static. In particular, Nancy finds the doctrine of the incarnation, of *homoousia* or consubstantiality, to be particularly rich for such ex-posures.[2]

Nancy wrestles intensely with incarnation in particular in his writings on Christianity. He recognizes that, by insisting upon the impossible gathering-together of God and a human being in the singular person of Christ, Christianity opens up, even against itself, a multiplicity and "trans/immanence" that cannot solidify into hegemony. According to Christian doctrine, Jesus Christ is both God *and* man, but in a single person; Christ has two "natures" and two "wills," but again, *is* singular—one body. Christ, as depicted, disseminated, and dissected in official Christian doctrine, is neither a ghost in a machine nor a simple disguise, for either of those approaches eliminates the singularity of his plurality.[3] Nancy directs his attention to the division of what cannot be divided—that this person, Jesus, is at one and the same time *both* God *and a* man—and exploits the opening or gap in which Christianity, as a system, undoes itself.

In this chapter, I work through Nancy's various interpolations of incarnation, from the negative pole in *Corpus* to the more nuanced approach found in *Dis-Enclosure*. In the second section, I review the early Church Fathers' hypotheses regarding the incarnation, culminating in the creeds of Nicea and Chalcedon. That the early Church Fathers were reliant upon Scripture and not philosophy per se, as earlier scholars assumed, opens up a world of interpretations.[4] I pay attention to the points of incongruence and paradox in the early patristics, reading them as moments of opening, places where incarnation can be read against itself so that it becomes a site of the opening and spacing of bodies rather than the site of their closure and suffocation.

This is not to say that the official teachings of the Church throughout history would be supportive of my reading—far from it. But I am less concerned with being orthodox, and more concerned with locating, expanding, and extrapolating said moments in order to perform work upon the Christian corpus, work that exposes this corpus. The sources of doctrine come from a multitude of texts, with a plurality of "Jesuses" and gods. This suggests that Nancy's thesis is correct, that Christianity does deconstruct itself in its very construction. To rely upon the multiple voices and bodies of Jesus to construct a doctrine of incarnation, a doctrine that does not capitulate to philosophical categories but again and again rejects the overtly philosophical for the messier multiplicity of natures, bodies, and paradoxes, indicates and indicts Christianity not as a tie that binds (*religio*), but rather as a saying that opens.

I then examine nineteenth and twentieth century theories of incarnation, including *kenosis* theology, where there is more resonance with Nancy's own unpacking of the language of incarnation and the a/theizing of God. Particularly in the work of John Macquarrie, we find a kenotic theology that avoids the metaphysical assumptions that plague Christian theology, Western monotheism, and Western hegemony. Finally, this chapter explores more marginal theologians in their attempts to problematize and open the body of Christ to a theology of bodies in and as the world. Such theologians are rarely found with the hallowed halls of divinity schools (although you can find some if you look carefully). Instead, theologians eager to rescue bodies from the history of the West often approach the texts and doctrines of Christianity from queer or marginal perspectives. Thus, the work of Cheri DiNovo and Craig Keen provide ways into the body of Christ that allow for openings to expose themselves. This chapter thus has three goals: one educational, one deconstructive, and one collaborative.

THE BODY IN INCARNATION: NANCY

Nancy addresses incarnation in several works: in *Corpus,* his manifesto of a coming ontology of the body, and in several essays in *Dis-Enclosure: The Deconstruction of Christianity.* His use and interpretation of the incarnation shifts from one work to the next. While in *Corpus,* Nancy views the motif of the incarnation negatively, as that which threatens an ontology of the body, in the essays of *Dis-Enclosure*, he finds the same motif more fruitful for its deconstructive possibilities. If the body of Christ as the incarnation haunts Western discourse and practice, while Christianity sows the seeds of its own deconstruction, then it is conducive to uncover those moments so that they may produce the unraveling we wish them to.

It should be noted from the outset that philosophers who have worked with Nancy's writings have made it clear that Nancy rejects the Christian doctrine of incarnation as a proper ontology of the body.[5] Daniele Rugo, for instance, argues briefly that "making-place" is better than "incarnation" as an articulation of the kind of ontology Nancy sets out to perform. B. C. Hutchens speaks more strongly, suggesting that Nancy has no truck in any theological structures: "The dangerous vacuity of theological speculation has the merit of offering consolations at the expense of free enquiry into the sense of freedom and community in particular."[6] It is true that the doctrine of incarnation, historically, preserves a dichotomy or duality of spirit and body that Nancy thinks should be undone. However, I will argue that he sets forth his own, non-religious, theory, just as he attempts to construct a nonreligious usage of resurrection.[7] While the doctrines of the Church, accepted without question, have no place in Nancy's world, the interrogation of those doctrines, uncovering their restless centers, is necessary if one wants to move toward what Nancy calls the *mundus corpus*: the world of bodies alone. It has also been claimed, rightly, that Nancy opposes incarnation as a trope or motif of the West, and sees in it a devaluing of the body in order to elevate the soul/spirit/transcendence.[8] Carefully parsing Nancy's deconstruction of incarnation provides us with a lens to approach the actual doctrines and theories of incarnation as they have been constructed, dismantled, and reorganized throughout the history of the West. To dismiss theological speculation as empty seems to undermine the very project Nancy is attempting to perform, for it is via theological speculation that Christianity exists in the first place, and thus we cannot deconstruct Christianity if we avoid its thinkers and doctrines, or dismiss them outright. If Christianity must in many ways deconstruct itself, it is necessary to assume its theology is not completely vacuous.

In *Corpus*, Nancy addresses incarnation as "where Spirit infuses the body," which is a too-simplistic and also inaccurate reflection of the doctrine(s) of the incarnation created and expanded on by Christian thinkers. Thinking through a Latin phrase of the Church, *verbum caro factum est* ("And the word became flesh"), Nancy demonstrates that there are two senses by which one may interpret this phrase, and that each excludes the other. In one sense, the flesh, the body, *caro,* "gives rise to the Word's glory and true coming," whereas the other sense prioritizes the Word (Logos) giving "rise to the true presence and sense of flesh."[9] Either the flesh opens for the Word, or the Word inaugurates, sanctifies, the flesh. Nancy's focus upon the opening passages of the Gospel of John (the "philosophical" Gospel) demonstrates that, rather than a holding-together in simultaneity of flesh and Logos, there is an absolute antecedence of the Principle (or Logos) from the beginning.[10] There is no "inter-space" left, as the Logos takes priority in this articulation. In short, the abstract, non-corporeal ideal or Idea (or Word) temporally precedes and ontologically exceeds the actual worldly body of Jesus. This privileges the idea over the body, and the abstract over the specific. Nancy expresses frustration at this, writing "even though the Gospel of the Nativity itself is here, or wants to be here," John's Gospel rules out beginning with the body, instead placing the beginning of the incarnation in a time immemorial and place Outside the world.[11] Rather than a gospel of spacing, John's Gospel is a gospel of temporality, of succession. Nancy points out: "The body is the penetration and progression of the principle into the darkness of what comes after, of what's kept beneath."[12]

Nancy appropriately relates this to Plato, as we hear echoes not only of a Christian Gentile prioritization of time over space but of spirit over body, with the body as nothing more than the tomb or prison of the soul. Nancy writes, "Incarnation causes the principle to penetrate the thing that obscures and obfuscates it."[13] The body muddies the intellectual waters; it hides or covers the spirit or soul. It is a trap, one that must be sprung (and unsprung). The body becomes a sign of imprisonment and interiority, a prison for that which was outside and now is within, and thus the body must expel the soul, the truth, from its hidden caverns.

It is this incarnational ontology that Nancy wishes to see dissolve. "Incarnation is structured like a disembodiment": by placing priority and value upon the principle or soul or spirit, one devalues the body, disembodies it of itself.[14] The body is merely a site of signification for a non-material soul or spirit that must make use of the body in order to cast it off.[15] In any case, Nancy proceeds with his evisceration of the incarnation:

> Spirit is the organ of sense, or the *true body*, the transfigured body. Here, then, the spirit of Christianity, meaning Christianity as a theology of the Holy Spirit, is entirely whole: a religion of breath (already Judaic), of impalpable touch, a religion of the Word, of proferring, of exhaling—a deleterious odor of the dead—a religion of expiration and inspiration, a general pneumatology, a religion of filiation: the Spirit passes from Father to Son (it's enough for the mother, for her part, to be an intact womb through which this breath will have passed); the son is the body, not the expansion that creates bodies, but the spirit's body, gathered up, concentrated in its breath, offered in sacrifice to the father it returns to by expiring, the body of the last cry, of the final sigh, where everything is consumed.[16]

In the end, for Nancy the incarnation leaves bodies as open wounds, torn apart by the exhalation of the spirit, abandoned. This is where the incarnation leaves its body.

It looks bad for the theory of the incarnation, from this perspective. The Western worldview of Christianity holds the body down as a site for the only *real* truth, the spirit. This theory of incarnation, ironically, is not of or for bodies—it does not *want* them. Rather, bodies are merely sites for breath, for spirit, to pass through on its way to somewhere else. The body of Christ becomes a way station, a place through which to pass, not an opening as such for bodies to be bodies, but instead a mere vehicle for an essential and inevitable passing-through that ends with the recollection of spirit to itself. This is a solid story—it is a way of making-sense. According to Nancy, it is also passing away, and Nancy does not mourn its passing in the slightest, although it may hurt to lose this solid ground, this single place/space (or the myth of it, at any rate).

Thus, in *Corpus*, Nancy unworks Western understandings of the body, arriving at a new "schematic" of the *body as sense-making*, as a breakthrough of sense into all the acts of interpretation and signification we perform.[17] The body does not allow the accretion of constructions, but rather ex-poses these constructions *as* it exists. It refuses stable sense-making, instead providing a loose movement of meaning-making that refuses to be sanctified by a Word from outside the world. Historically, the (monotheistic, imperialist) 'West' has utilized its own religious utterances (including the liturgy of the Eucharist: "This is my body") to establish a totality, a closed, completed body. Nancy, on the other hand, seeks to reveal the body as the site where "*This...*'" is displaced.[18]

Nancy views the world contrary to the dualistic view of Western monotheism. The world does not consist of matter and spirit, or soul and body, or even ego and body, but bodies all the way down—a "world of the outside. The world of outsides."[19] Rather than spirit breaking in or infusing matter, the outside of the world is *in* the world, *as* others' bodies, and as my own body, which is other to myself even as it is myself. We are not monadic in our experience of being ourselves. Even our parts have parts, our senses are disjointed, and we are in the process of decomposing. This worldview Nancy labels *mundus corpus*, a world of bodies. In attempting to begin this discourse of *mundus corpus*, Nancy recognizes the inevitable failures and limits: bodies, in their vulnerabilities and openness, are nevertheless strangely inviolable, impenetrable by discourse and analysis and thought. Yet he resists mightily turning this *mundus corpus* into a kind of mysticism that would allow us to elevate this mysterious, close-as-a-touch body to an Other, ineffable and sublime. Nancy is resolute that even our thinking must remain here-now: "It may be that all entries into all bodies . . . have disappeared with the body of God—and perhaps we're left only with the *corpus* of anatomy, biology, and mechanics. But even this, and precisely this, means: *here*, the world of bodies . . . and *there*, a cut off, incorporeal discourse."[20]

Nancy provides, then, his own sketch of an ontology-to-come, where bodies are not traps and caverns but open sites of sense, sensing, and meaning. Adopting a tone reminiscent of Jacques Derrida, Nancy intimates that bodies are the coming, the coming that never ends, because what is, is the present: constantly arriving and always local. Bodies arrive, bloody in birth, and are on the move from that moment. Bodies create space in their movement, in their living-out. What is essential to bodies is not materiality or substance, but the making of space. Thus, in Nancy's ontology, the creation of the body is not according to some ideal or image—we are not made in the image of God. There is no prior blueprint. What comes to be in a world of bodies is the *space* of those bodies, those bodies as spacing.[21] Bodies are what allow spacing to be, for bodies are exterior; however, this exteriority does not imply its obverse, interiority, but rather the dichotomy shifts, from interior/exterior to exterior/world. It is a shift that keeps shifting, however, as bodies are what the world *is*—there is not a strict ontological difference between my body and this world I occupy.

If bodies are exteriors that expose themselves and make up the world, then the concept of God must undergo a radical shift as well. Playing against the traditional theories of incarnation, Nancy suggests that God is not substance, but *mode*—and the world is not a world of substance, but of *modalities*. If bodies are not closed substances—shells that hide interior souls—then God, too, in Western discourse, undoes Godself, and becomes something other than a Spirit-Being outside the world. If our inherited narrative claims that God created *limon* (dust), made the body out of it, and then became that kind of body, then in becoming *that body*, God altered his *mode*. Rather than God being one Substance, and Matter another, God becomes a *mode* of bodies. In Nancy's ontology, what *matters* is not substance, but modality itself. Nancy's bodies are modes and rhythms rather than substances—they come and go, decay and rise, touch and touch themselves. Creation and existence consist of this ontological dance of bodies. He poses this against the substantialist doctrine of incarnation, which he describes as "the other, [and] the same, indiscernible *and* distinct, coupled as in love."[22]

We can further see Nancy's critique of incarnation in his essay, "On the Soul," also found in the English translation of *Corpus*. Building on his earlier analysis of the incarnation as the reduction of flesh to signifying substance, and spirit as animating Otherness penetrating and using the body then abandoning it, Nancy defines spirit in this essay as concentration or mass (both of which are negative terms in his ontology). "Mass" is closed, concentrated, impenetrable. So too is spirit, in that it is unassailable as a concept, unable to be opened because it is dimensionless, it takes up no space. Instead of spirit, Nancy revives and redefines "soul" as the *outside* of the body, the opening or openness of the body *as* body, or as "body's difference from itself, the relation to the outside that the body is for itself."[23] He acknowledges the Platonic and Christian overtones of reviving the term "soul," and also acknowledges that the traditions there are more "complex than it seems."[24] Nevertheless, he is resolute in his rejection of incarnation as a thematic structure, based upon his negative analysis of it in *Corpus*. Thus, he concludes:

> We can in no way think of the body in terms of incarnation. I am speaking not only of the Christian dogma of incarnation, *where that which is without place, without exteriority, without form, with matter (God) comes into flesh*, but of the incarnation that is the model (itself Christian, in effect) of all our thought on the subject. This idea of incarnation is impossible: what does it mean that something without place would come to occupy a place? It isn't a question, then, of being there. Rather, it has to do with . . . "being the there."[25]

Nancy presents a strident and Johannine presentation of the incarnation in *Corpus*. Relying heavily upon the Logos language in the Gospel of John, and pulling (perhaps inadvertently) from the Logos theology once fancied but then rejected by the early Church, Nancy constructs the incarnation as the penetration of matter by spirit, with a subsequent ontological reduction of body to a signifying placeholder for the real agent, "spirit." Certainly, the Gospel of John lends itself to such a reading. However, to focus entirely upon this gospel for one's theory of incarnation risks oversimplifying incarnation theories, flattening them and making of them straw men to dispose of quickly. In moving so quickly from a Johannine view of incarnation to its condemnation, we risk losing moments of deconstructive possibility.

As we approach the incarnation in the essays of *Dis-Enclosure*, however, we find some significant shifts in Nancy's thought. In "A Faith That Is Nothing at All," Nancy opens up Gérard Granel's own thinking on incarnation and faith. A term missing throughout *Corpus*—*kenosis*—makes an appearance here. Nancy interprets Granel's turn away from religion as one that reserves the term "divine" to describe the opening of the world to *itself*, rather than an opening of the world to or by some outside, formless Other. It is *kenosis* thinking taken to its extreme conclusion. Nancy writes, "What remains of the divine . . . would be this name *dies/divus*, which would gather in itself a *kenosis* wherein a/theology would come to show itself as destitution and the truth of the 'mystery.'"[26] Granel himself arrives at the incarnation without God—if by God we mean the God of the Other who descends, condescends, penetrates, and assumes the property of the flesh. Granel provides an incarnational thinking that resists the history of Western thought.

Nancy points out an eliding or slippage of terms Granel evokes in his elliptical conclusion: Granel moves from a notion of creation as the opening of the world *as* the world, to the more traditional notion of "the fable of a product supposed to produce without material."[27] Nancy points out that this slippage is provocative, because "Either God empties himself of himself in the opening of the world, or God sustains himself as being, by himself, subject and substance of the world. It is not at all the same 'God' here." Granel may dismiss the onto-theological God, but:

> he does not dismiss a god emptying himself of God. . . . But this divine of exhaustion is precisely that of *kenosis*, whose mark or emblem this text carries. By the same token, the change in sign for *kenosis*—bearing an ontological, and no longer theological sign—proves to be an operation less simple than it might appear. We cannot avoid asking why he has recourse to the Pauline term . . .[28]

In other words, Granel leaves behind a remainder. By evoking, vocalizing, the Pauline term *kenosis*, Granel leaves the door open to the theological even when he insists he has moved to the ontological alone.

The god of the philosophers is not the god emptied in *kenosis*. Firstly, *kenosis* suggests changeability and passivity, but the god of the philosophers is Being itself, unchangeable and impassable. Nancy coins a term for Granel's philosophical thought, *almost* emptied of theological content: kenology. "A kenology would have placed him under a summons to state what happens to the logos therein."[29] Nancy suggests a path that may involve "a paradoxical fulfillment of Christianity in its own exhaustion," even as he (Nancy) himself may reject it.[30]

In the *Dis-Enclosure* essays, Nancy also reprises his summative rejection of the incarnation found in *Corpus*—but he rejects such a summation as nondoctrinal. The Christian *credo* does not claim a spirit-possession, but rather a change in substance: God was *made* flesh, *became* a body. The body of Jesus, then, is not simply a location for the soul (or God), a suit of flesh put upon by the ineffable Spirit. Rather, "The logos itself . . . makes itself body as Logos . . ."[31] If God is that which "puts himself outside himself," is this not an echoing, linguistically, of how Nancy understands the relation of body/soul in *Corpus*? This intimates a thinking-ahead from within Christianity toward a transimmanent body. Monotheism, as an atheism, performs precisely what Nancy thinks is so necessary for a material ontology of the body—a loss of presence, of foundation, of external founding of the world. Here is where Nancy's firm rejection of incarnation in *Corpus* takes a different tone: "The body of the incarnation is the place, or rather the taking place, the event, of that disappearance."[32] Rather than simply jettisoning the idea of the incarnation as irredeemably dangerous, a reification of body/spirit dichotomies that reduces bodies to mere signifiers, Nancy suggests a more kenotical understanding of incarnation, whereby God-as-Outside and Other disappears. This disappearing, this death of God, is what Nancy aims for. God incarnate is a spacing, which is precisely the ontological thinking Nancy is working toward. The body incarnate becomes a *syncope*, a beat, an event, a break-in that joins the body to itself and to other bodies in a multiplicity.

The incarnation opens an unraveling of this concept of God, so much so that God becomes gesture, not being; becomes a movement of passing, a passage. Nancy in several essays uses *syncope* to indicate a beating, a rhythm, a pulsing, that is different, that is gesture, that is God as the "Unnameable, nonmeaningful" signal that does not signify anything at all.[33] Echoing, too, his use of the term "some*one*" to indicate the non-unity, non-duality of body/soul in or as a person, Nancy uses "someone" to indicate that someone indeed passes—a "who," not a "what." "The name God, or that way of saying the god of someone (The God of Akhenaton, the God of Abraham, of Isaac, and of Jacob, the God of Jesus Christ, the God of Muhammad, and also 'my God,' the God of myself, a God in each case mine) . . ."[34] The incarnate body is a syncope; the god who passes is a syncope; the god who passes is someone; I am someone, you are someone—and to speak of identity, or substance, with regard to any of these nouns, proper or common, is to fall back upon a dying ontology that needs, itself, to pass.

"Passing" is an interesting, loaded term in English. One passes a kidney stone; one passes someone on the freeway. One passes on an opportunity. We get a pass, give a pass, pass a class. We pass along. We pass away. In every case, passing contains a pervasive temporality that will not be shooed away. Nevertheless, Nancy wishes to remain thinking spatially here, not temporally (lest we fall back into thinking Being as Event). Passing for Nancy is movement: motion from one place to another, passing into and out of another place. Movement also involves displacing, and an inevitable disappearing. To think of the god of passing as incarnational may help clarify the deconstruction of the incarnation. In the incarnation, God atheologizes godself by self-emptying; God does not *possess* the flesh of a man, but *becomes* flesh and in so doing empties "God" of all radically alterior, anterior signification. If one is not describing an actual event but an event of thought—an event of thought that nevertheless has real effects on real bodies in their plurality and vulnerability—then in the thinking of the incarnation, one thinks an absent, empty "God." One approaches the throne to find it empty, or finds no throne at all. One looks for Being and finds a feeble body of a Jewish peasant, one that will die, with gaping wounds, vulnerable and opened by and to weapons, be they swords or words, a body that then is laid down in the tomb. The thinking of the incarnation gestures toward a God who does not exist outside of this bloody, fecal world of bodies, and who does not exist *inside* this world, either. At best, the thinking of the incarnation is a thinking of this world as multiple, as diverse, as an array of fleshes both insurmountably lonely and as close as touch. Nancy's rejection of the incarnation does not also entail rejection of the *thinking* of incarnation—for this thinking, all thinking, he tells us in *Corpus* and *Adoration*, is a kind of praying, and a kind of faith "that is nothing at all."[35]

There is a marked shift, then, between *Corpus* and the essays of *Dis-Enclosure* with regard to the thinking of the incarnation, although this shift does not in any substantial way alter Nancy's overall trajectory toward an ontology of bodies. This shift can, and for our purposes should, reflect upon the multiple articulations of the incarnation found in Christian thought. The incarnation is not monolithic, any more than Christianity is. Whereas the incarnation of the Gospel of John is redolent with philosophical bugbears, resulting in a kind of spirit-appropriation of flesh, in *kenosis* theology one finds a rather different sketching of the body of Christ. While Nancy is in no way arguing for one theology over against another, nor is he participating in the adolescent rejection of all things Christian, or treating Christian thought as a disease.[36] We find dis-enclosure even in systems that resolutely wish to remain closed; but, outrageously, in the systems of Christianity, we find no such resoluteness, but rather a habit of thought, flawed or doomed as it may be, to a radical openness. Nancy's understanding or thinking of the body is prefigured, introduced like a parasite come to devour its host, in Christian dogma regarding the body of God. Therefore, spending some time with different views of the incarnation in Christian thought, knowing them better, provides us with the opportunity to capitalize on such openings, such that the stranglehold of Western discourse may release the body from its grasp, setting it down with a touch, and allowing it to be free.

EARLY CHURCH CHRISTOLOGY

> He who makes rich is made poor; he takes on the poverty of my flesh, that I may gain the riches of his divinity. He who is full is made empty; he is emptied for a brief space of his glory, that I may share in his fullness.
> —St. Gregory the Nazianzen

Gregory the Nazianzen addressed the incarnation by echoing the kenosis of Christ, found in Paul's letter to the Philippians.[37] Paul wrote that Jesus, ". . . who, though he was in the form of God, did not regard equality with God as something to be exploited, but emptied himself, taking the form of a slave, being born in human likeness. And being found in human form, he humbled himself and became obedient to the point of death—even death on a cross."[38] Indeed, most articulations of the incarnation repeat similar language: the Other has been brought in, the most high has been brought low. But notice the passive language in the text above from Gregory. Rather than God as the actor, God is the subject, subjected, is receiving rather than doing. He is "made empty; he is emptied." In this emptiness, space is made for other bodies, and this is the hope of the incarnation. That "God so loved the world" creates a dichotomy of inside/outside, to be sure. However, that God entered the world, became subjected to it, became part of it, undoes or at least confuses the strict binary. What was separated, eternally and ontologically, is now joined. The doctrine of the incarnation, as it was eventually accepted by churches both East and West, claims that this was no mere "flesh-suit," nor simply an illusion, but rather that God was ontologically made flesh, made into a body. While many Christian thinkers tend toward a soul/body dualism that makes tempting the above heresies, one can see in Gregory's astounded articulation that what struck the early Church Fathers was the reality that God subjects himself to limits, to poverty, to emptiness.

It is important to note, however, that this emptiness is the sheer fact of God taking on a human body, not of abandoning His divine attributes. The notion of the abandon of God in the kenosis of Christ comes later in Christian history. The early Church, influenced as it was by the Platonists, still held to the impassable Eternal God; as such, the sheer idea that such a God would become flesh was kenosis enough.

However, a problem emerges in Christian thought: that of the two natures of Christ. Cyril of Alexandria provides the most succinct examples for this debate:

> God the Word full by nature and in every way Perfect, and distributing *out of His own Fullness* His own goods to the creature, *we say was emptied*: in no wise wronged in His own Proper Nature, nor changed so as to become otherwise, nor made in ought inferior, for inconvertible and unchangeable is Himself also even as He Who begat Him, and *never may He be capable of passion.* But when He was made Flesh, i.e. Man, He made (as He said, *I will pour forth of My Spirit upon all flesh*) the poverty of human nature His own; first, in that He was once made man, albeit He remained God; next in that He took the form of a servant, Who is in His own Nature free, as Son, and while He is Himself the Lord of glory He is said to receive glory: Himself Life, He is said to be quickened: and receives power over all, Himself King of all and with God, and He was obedient to the Father, suffered the Cross and so on. But these things befit the measure of the human nature, yet He makes them His own with flesh and fulfills the economy, remaining what He was.[39]

Cyril attempts to maintain the Otherness of God in Christ, insisting upon God's impassible nature, his inability to be affected. Nevertheless, he too cannot avoid the language of emptying and poverty. While God "chose" this path, the ontological reality of Christ-in-the-flesh was that of a man who could, indeed, suffer. Medieval theologians up through Thomas Aquinas struggled with this philosophical debate: If God is changeless (one can hear the echoes of the *Phaedo* and other works here, which equate changelessness with invisibility, uniformity with ideality), then how could God be made to suffer? To suffer is to change emotional states, and God cannot change without thereby being composite and therefore not eternal, not perfect, etc.

What is remarkable about this kind of onto-theology, prefigured here in Cyril, is that it is reductive regarding God's nature. God's nature must obey the rational precepts human minds have constructed. But to value unity over diversity is a philosophical move, put forth by Parmenides forward—it is not scriptural.[40] From the creation account to the plurality of the Gospels, Scripture describes a deity who values literal diversity (or multiversity), and who is understood in Trinitarian fashion already in early Christian thought. Therefore the emphasis upon uniformity, unicity, and changelessness smack of a neo-Platonism far more than of the "God of Abraham, Isaac and Jacob."[41]

Against Cyril was Archbishop Nestorius, whose position was later declared heretical. He is important for our purposes because he expressed what has come to be a common point of view among lay Christians. He held to a strict distinction between the two natures of Christ, human and divine. Like Cyril, Nestorius was concerned to maintain the divine nature of God as that which cannot change, suffer, etc. Thus, only the human aspect of Jesus could be said to suffer, to be born, to grow up, to be tortured, to weep, etc. If the divine nature of Christ could intervene and shield him from the experiences of being human, then he was not fully participating in what it is to be human. However, in his very attempt to prevent an illusionist understanding while retaining the absolute divinity of God, Nestorius actually affirms a mask-wearing Christ. He uses the word *prosopon* to describe the relationship between the two natures. *Prosopon* translates as "mask" and refers to the accouterments worn by Greek actors. It was later appropriated by Christian doctrine to mean "person" and to help articulate the Trinity.[42] So, and this gets into nuts and bolts few care about, Nestorius says there are two *natures* in Christ, united in one *person* (*prosopon*).

Cyril of Alexandria's position won the day. Yet what we find in them, in spite of his Platonist leanings, suggests a paradoxical character to the incarnation. He writes that the incarnation manifests ". . . the wound and its medicine, the sickness and the physician, what has been laid down in death and the one who raises to life . . "[43] This underscores the tensions that existed in many of the early Church's attempts to wrestle with the impossibility of the incarnation. On the one hand, philosophical influences, particularly of the neo-Platonists, urged early theologians toward a comprehensive and cogent account of the nature of God as such; on the other hand, Scripture's diversity and symbolic language called for them to find some way to articulate a *mystery*. This is good news, in that the Church Fathers failed to present a closed, coherent, systematic theology of the incarnation. Instead, we find openings and maneuvers, shifts in lingo and borrowings—a pastiche of philosophy and Scripture that leaves us room to breathe.

Then we come to the Council at Chalcedon (451). The Church at this time was avidly opposed to any doctrine that creates a hybrid God-man or a third kind of being who is neither/nor. Somehow, church leaders must insist on what was rationally impossible: they must preserve the notion that two natures reside in a single human being, Jesus Christ. The Chalcedonian Creed reads:

> . . . the same Son, our Lord Jesus Christ, the same perfect in Godhead and also perfect in manhood; truly God and truly man, of a reasonable [rational] soul and body; consubstantial [co-essential] with the Father according to the Godhead, and consubstantial with us according to the Manhood; in all things like unto us, without sin; begotten before all ages of the Father according to the Godhead, and in these latter days, for us and for our salvation, born of the Virgin Mary, the Mother of God, according to the Manhood; one and the same Christ, Son, Lord, only begotten, to be acknowledged in two natures, inconfusedly, unchangeably, indivisibly, inseparably; the distinction of natures being by no means taken away by the union, but rather the property of each nature being preserved, and concurring in one Person (*prosopon*) and one Subsistence (*hypostasis*), not parted or divided into two persons, but one and the same Son, and only begotten God,the Word, the Lord Jesus Christ; as the prophets from the beginning [have declared] concerning Him, and the Lord Jesus Christ Himself has taught us, and the Creed of the holy Fathers has handed down to us.[44]

The Chalcedonian Confession claimed two natures, inextricably connected and yet distinct, possessing full divinity and full humanity at one and the same time, forming one person (Jesus). This creed was, more than anything else, a compromise position between the two extremes presented by Nestorius and Cyril. This proved an impossible compromise, as the two positions being held were irreconcilable.

Thus, a third early Church Father provided a way forward. Athanasius, an Egyptian theologian opposed to Arianism, wrote:

> Come now . . . let us...relate also the things concerning the Incarnation of the Word . . . which the Jews slander and the Greeks mock, but we ourselves venerate, so that, all the more from his apparent degradation, you may have an even greater and fuller piety towards him, for the more he is mocked by unbelievers by so much he provides a greater witness of his divinity, because *what human beings cannot understand as impossible, these he shows to be possible*. . . . So, rightly wishing to help human beings, *he sojourned as a human being, taking to himself a body like theirs and from below—I mean through the works of the body*. . . . *[He] dwells as human among humans and draws to himself the perceptible senses of all human beings...* [45]

Athanasius' account, as found in *On the Incarnation of the Word*, ended up determining doctrinal positions regarding the incarnation's purposes and meaning. Athanasius understood the incarnation as a necessary act of God due to human beings' enslavement not to sin, but to the wages of sin: death. Athanasius argued that only God can defeat death, but must defeat death by himself dying—and yet, God cannot die. Only in this trickery can the devil be defeated and death lose its sway. While the bulk of his argument is unpersuasive, he presented a few intriguing propositions with regard to the current project: First and foremost, that God can make possible the impossible. This is tacit acknowledgment, contra his own logic, that the Eternal becoming Finite is, theoretically speaking, impossible. So is the death of the undying, Eternal God. Athanasius draws our attention almost unwittingly to the paradox of the God-man, even though such language will not be used for centuries.

Athanasius proved his paradoxical point via the use of *communicatio idiomatum* (the communication of properties), whereby one argues for similarities between two distinct things such that both share in the similitude. As body and soul are united yet distinct (the argument goes), so too was Jesus the *Logos* and flesh (*sarx*) at the same time, not intermixed but so intimately tied together that what happens to one, happens to the other: "The divine Logos could suffer in the flesh, and the flesh of the Logos could become the firstborn of the dead."[46] The God of the philosophers, who cannot suffer, is sacrificed to the God of the incarnation, who can and does. God is rent asunder.

This is a good time to pause and reflect on what emerges from a quick scan of early church debates regarding the incarnation. First, Nancy is right to call out and reject the ontological dualism that projects God as an Outside Eternal Other founding the world, who penetrates this world by taking on flesh in Christ. We see the impasse this produces for early Christology. It is logically unsolvable—it requires a spirit-ontology that places the origin of the world in a Beyond, and, at its worst, it relativizes the world and the bodies that make up the world by reducing bodies to mere signifiers or placeholders for Spirit.

And yet. In the midst of these attempts to explain exactly how God became (a) man, intractable problems arise, and the solutions to these problems—the solvent that should dissolve them—instead holds them open. In rejecting more rational or philosophical explanations for the incarnation, the church instead preserved, codified, and cemented the open, wounded body of God, who, in an act of emptying (or in our act of thinking it) "atheolozies" Godself. Precisely at the place where church teaching becomes dogma, the doctrine "surrected"—set up—is one that empties the world of God.

Let us examine, then, a subset of early Christology, Logos theology, which was later rejected by the church. The early Church jettisoned the monist, unmoved mover or Eternal Form of the God of the Greek philosophers, the very heart of monotheism. While later medievalists resurrect the Greeks, and certainly the church struggles with their ghosts, church dogma holds to a far more paradoxical and kenotic understanding of God in Christ.

Second-century Christians borrowed heavily from Greek philosophy in order to think through the possibilities of the opening passage of John's Gospel, and since this is the Gospel Nancy references most, it is worth a brief foray. *Logos*' dual meaning as both "reason" and "speech" opened up possibilities for the relation between God and Jesus for early Christians. *Logos* was the Reason or Order that structured the universe; it also became a sort of demiurge for Middle Platonists struggling to understand how an eternally transcendent unchanging principle, like the Form of the Good, could have to do with changeable materiality in any way. From a monotheistic point of view, this *Logos* issues from God: It is the thought of God ex-pressed as creation, particularly the creation of the world.[47] Thus, early Christian thinkers borrowed heavily from the Platonists in their theological arguments.

One problem with this definition, from a Christological as well as monotheistic perspective, is that Logos theology seems to set up two gods, one subordinate to the other. By suggesting that God acts via *Logos*, a kind of demiurge or force that does the real work of interacting with the material world, Logos theology imports an excess of Platonism into Christian theology. Origen, therefore, argues that Logos theology (1) derives too much from philosophy rather than *Scripture;* and (2) emphasizes Logos over all the other metaphors used for Jesus in Scripture, thus giving it too much definitive power. Logos theology was ultimately abandoned for Origen's argument of relation based in part upon Greek philosophical categories. Origen argues first from a categorical perspective (Aristotle's category of relation is helpful here).[48] In order for an object to be understood as having a particular quality in the category of relation, another object must be referenced to complete the relation: a relation always requires two. The typical example is precisely that of familial relation: one is only a "mother" if one has (or has had) a son, for example. If God is to be understood *from eternity* as the "father," then there must have always-already been a "son" in order for the relation to stand and the category to hold. Origen also tried to bolster this view by examining the verb tense used in the opening passages of the Gospel of John. The verb is in the past tense: "In the beginning *was* the Logos . . ." This does not imply that Jesus Christ "came to be," but rather simply *was,* before the beginning of the world.[49] We see Origen's influence in the Nicene Creed, established by council in 325 CE.[50] This early tendency among some Church leaders to philosophize God in Christ contributes to the onto-theological, philosophical accounts of the later medievalists. However, we find that not every early Church thinker was wedded to philosophy; and even if they were, strange alchemy results when one brings philosophy to the body of Christ.

MODERN THEOLOGY

Out of necessity, this chapter does not attempt to present every theologian who ever thought about the incarnation, but rather attempts to locate, within the broader Western canon of theology, arguments or perspectives that shed light on the auto-deconstructive elements in Christianity. This brings us to *kenosis* models for incarnation. While the early Church Fathers understood *kenosis* to be the *initial*, entirely humiliating act of God becoming flesh, nineteenth century theologians (Søren Kierkegaard among them) suggested that the way forward was to see *kenosis* as God's self-limiting in Christ: that God voluntarily gave up his relational attributes (omniscience, etc.) while retaining his "immanent" ones (holiness, truth, etc.).[51] This had the effect of relativizing God, however, and essentially eliminating His divinity: If God's attributes are so easily separated, the very unity that philosophical constructs claim for God is lost. God becomes composite. Yet here we have the seeds of a *nonreligious incarnational theology*. While rejected as unorthodox for logical and soteriological reasons, nevertheless theologians of good will argued that the incarnation "was a transformation of the Logos into human soul," an "abandonment" of divinity.[52] This language places us in familiar territory regarding Nancy's work. That theologians from within Lutheran orthodoxy (in Germany) attempt such a thing is audacious, and should give us a bit of depth historically when we read Nancy's articulations of the same. If anything, Nancy's nonreligious theology has some roots in *kenosis* theology—this may be the only version of Christian theology that could work with his reading of incarnation, because it is the only version that (ostensibly) erases God. Again, to say that Nancy is against incarnation is to only be partially correct. As the starting point for a theory of *bodies*, incarnation theologies that import the Spirit of God into human flesh are bad news. But as a way of deconstructing Christianity, the *kenosis* theology of the nineteenth century is helpful indeed.

It is in the twentieth century that we find the richest accounting of kenotic theology against the doctrine set forth at Chalcedon. Rather than proceeding from a philosophical definition of God and then working to understand the incarnation while preserving God's essential attributes, kenotic theology reflects the early twentieth-century turn to a historical account of Jesus as the source for Christological thought. We find in the work of Paul Tillich and others a focus upon the historical person of Jesus as a man who surrenders himself and empties himself completely so as to open the way to, or even literally embody, the love of God for the world. Such kenotic theology, in the words of John Macquarrie, "want[s] to make sense of Christology without appealing to mythological or metaphysical ideas."[53] Such theories also resist the latent Docetism of even Chalcedon.[54] Macquarrie points out that these theologies are, technically speaking, heretical, in that they hold to an adoptionist view of Jesus, whereby he was fully human and only subsequently and at the end of his life adopted into the personhood of God. But by focusing upon an *existential* account of Christ rather than (as the early Church does) an *ontological* account, *kenosis* theology avoids the difficulties the early church faced, but also cedes ontological ground, essentially proving Nancy's point that incarnation is not good ontology, or really ontology at all.

However, Macquarrie does not accept this limitation completely. Rather, he wishes to retain both adoptionism and incarnationism. He therefore does try to come at *kenosis* ontologically. However, this brings back exactly what Nancy seeks to avoid—God as Being. He writes, "Our God is not some unchanging monolith, but the God who pours out being and confers being upon a world."[55] The first path toward a recovery of ontology in *kenosis* leads Macquarrie back to Logos theology, this time rebranded for a modern era. He argues, "Creation is already a self-emptying, a self-giving and self-spending on the part of God," thus grounding a definition of God *as* self-giving and self-emptying. This is more helpful ontologically speaking, in that it echoes Nancy's a/theology. Nevertheless, it retains the dualism of World/God, the transcendence v. immanence Nancy finds so destructive. Even if "creation has been revealed as self-emptying," the initiator-God who sets it all in motion is retained.

A second path in *kenosis* theology suggests that Christ is not so much "firstborn of God" as "firstborn of all creation," the very model of creation, the exemplar. Macquarrie moves to a more ethical reading of the *kenosis* of Christ here, arguing that Christ modeled the proper way of all creation: All creation is designed to manifest in an outpouring of "creative love," and Jesus opens the way or is the pinnacle of that rightly-ordered excessive emptying. This may resonate well with the rather explicit concern for an ethic in Nancy's philosophy. Nancy's work toward a new ontology of bodies is no mere academic exercise, but rather an attempt to open a way of "being-with" that is more human, and more humane, than the dominance of Western metaphysics. Thus, from an ethical perspective, *kenosis* theology offers a companion piece to Nancy's own work.

We find both resonance and dissonance in exploring kenotic theology through a Nancean lens. On the one hand, the move away from a metaphysical reduction of God to a philosophical concept, toward a humanist rendering of incarnation as *kenosis*, potentially loosens the grip of onto-theology and creates space for thinking God otherwise. This allows for a deconstructive rendering of *kenosis* in which God disappears, passes by, is made absent, thus allowing the thinking of an ontology of bodies that no longer relies upon an invisible Guarantor. On the other hand, because it is theology, onto-theology tends to slip in the back door, manifesting itself as *kenosis* theology, but nevertheless quietly insisting that God-as-Being is Present, even if it is in a paradoxical articulation (emptying rather than fulfillment; weakness rather than omnipotence, etc.) *Kenosis* theology wants to eat its cake and have it too, to be "modern" and not so fusty as those Being-obsessed Church Fathers, yet maintain nevertheless a loyalty toward a Being who stands outside the world. A Being who loves the world *into* being still relativizes the existence of the world in doing so. While Nancy is not against the contingency and fragility of our existence together, it is a contingency between us, created, maintained, and fractured by us, not one that is guaranteed or set in motion by an Other. As such, incarnation theories still fail, ultimately, to sufficiently empty themselves of God.

Marginal Incarnation

I am not ready to give up yet, however, on incarnation and Nancy. Deconstructing certain creeds of Christianity and passages of Scripture reveals how an articulation of the possibility of the ontological body gets started: *this* body, the body of Christ, multiple in its singularity, making god absent by its very existence, is at the same time that which articulates the being of our bodies, together. Nancy's usage of *kenosis* opens up the possibility of conversation with other postmodern theologians on the margins. As theologian Craig Keen puts it, "The love of God that empties itself and moves into what God is not, into God's other, is precisely the love to which *we* are called."[56] The *kenosis* of God as Christ, which atheologizes God and opens up the locus of the body as the site of the world, is also the *kenosis* of Christian love, whereby one is to do the impossible—one is to give the self one does not possess to the other, to every other.

Craig Keen is a figure on the margins of what Mark Lewis Taylor calls the "guild" of theology. Rather late in life, he has published two books (so far) of collected essays and addresses, most of them given at various conferences or as chapel addresses at American Christian colleges. He is not employed by a top-tier divinity school, and his work is only now, after a lifetime of teaching, getting recognition. As such, I feel pretty comfortable referring to him as "marginal." One finds in Keen's work an echo of Nancy's, albeit from a theological perspective. Like Nancy, Keen wishes to see undone or laid to rest the hegemonic hope in a Supreme Being that "the world of beings stands in relation to . . . the divine Ground."[57] Such a Being values unification, security, and wholeness as opposed to multiplicities, vulnerabilities, and openness. Against this supreme ontology, Keen places the abasement of Jesus as the abasement of God. Jesus is a "poor peasant girl's helpless baby of uncertain legitimacy . . . homeless."[58] "God" in the synoptic narratives does not remain aloof and inviolable, but precisely descends, opens the closed world of beings, and comes "for the poor and diseased and outcast and frail, for the lost and forgotten, for the dying and the dead and the damned."[59] While Keen also retains the language of Otherness, the language of the outside breaking in, he nevertheless maintains a Kierkegaardian orientation to the abased condition of the life of Jesus, thus emphasizing not the philosophical Supreme Being but a broken, fragmented, vulnerable God. And, while we will reserve an elaboration of resurrection for another chapter, it is worthwhile to note that the abased Jesus continues in his abasement postresurrection: "his stripes are not healed; he remains the lamb slain."[60]

Keen writes:

> Without the loss of his human nature or his human will, without the loss of his human heart or soul or mind or strength, without the loss of his human ignorance or weakness or vulnerability, that is, without the loss of his 'flesh,' Jesus becomes that human life which is the concrete movement of God into the world. . . . *Here human being is opened to God and God is opened to human being.*[61]

This ex-pression of the incarnation may be the best we can hope for from within Christian thought, without said thinking losing its Christian orientation in an empty humanism. While it will not satisfy those who seek to expulse God from discourse, or those who seek to preserve hard-won terrain in the battle against theology, post-modern theologians such as Keen open theology to its own machinations, exposing the particular body of Jesus that resides in its heart, a body that explodes the closure of the world. Rather than a God of integrity established as our property, our proper way of being, or as something outside that determines us in that being, Keen reads the revelation of God in Christ as an openness in which we participate. There is nothing left of God outside of Jesus Christ—no reserved essence left untouched by the world. As such, Keen boldly claims, against both more traditional theologians and against the flattening simplification often applied to Christianity by those outside it, "there is little in the doctrine of the Trinity that resonates with hierarchical Western metaphysics, with onto-theology, with the ontology of the Supreme Being."[62] In other words, he echoes Nancy's thesis: Christianity deconstructs itself from within its own Scriptures, dogmas, and doctrines.

Queer Theology

Turning to queer theology may also provide fruitful ground for thinking incarnation deconstructively. First, a quick definition: Queer theology is not a social-political critique of moral norms as established by church and state, although it may lead to such a critique. Moreover, it stands outside and "slantward" to even such hetero-normative movements as the gay marriage movement, in that gay marriage reifies and accepts as desirable the normativity of a binary marital construction. Rather, queer theology aims at expressing that which is "strange or odd from a conventional viewpoint."[63] Drawing from queer theorists such as Judith Butler, who defines "queer" as "a site of collective contestation . . . never fully owned, but always and only redeployed, twisted, queered from a prior usage . . .," queer theology sets itself in the midst of this ongoing interrogation not only into the established norms of theology and the church, but into the term "queer" itself as a potential site of reification and closure.[64]

Cheri DiNovo is one such "queer theologian," who rejects ontology, and does so *via* Scripture. She writes, in her scan on the Gospel of John in *Qu(e)erying Evangelism: Growing Community from the Outside In*:

> [Jesus] is certainly not of this world. But of what world is he? He is sent by someone from whom he is never, in a sense, separate. There is an undecidability, a rift in the very core of this God. . . . John's Jesus both points away from himself to the Father but also to himself as one with the Father, both to the one who sent him and to himself as the Ontological One. He is both/and. He is both the originary and points to a more prior originary. In this way, he claims originary as Derrida would understand it. But unlike Derrida, he claims it originarily. He is strange, odd, weird, unusual, unique, queer. John's Jesus turns the tables.[65]

In the Gospel of Luke, DiNovo sees Jesus as one who chooses to live as and in human, mortal temporality, and therefore does so *completely*. Regarding the Gospel of Matthew, she writes, "A Jesus who is one with the Father calls out to the Father. The wounded Jesus calls out through the ink of a wounded text. There is slippage at the heart of the one we call God; our God is pierced, wounded. *What God has rent asunder, no human can put back together.*"⁶⁶ Continuing:

> Jesus Christ may represent a break in God as ontological truth, a God both human and divine that qu(e)eries everything we thought we knew about a removed, omnipotent master of the universe. In Derridean terms, Jesus Christ may represent a break in the economy of the circle or a birthplace of the economy. Jesus Christ may represent a God of differánce. Jesus Christ may be the call from the whirlwind, a call against God as ontology or ontologies, a call to love as faith, as giving the economy of the gift its chance . . .⁶⁷

DiNovo suggests that Jesus, "in being the true human and truly Divine, in being the queer beginning of queerness," rather than being someone able to be codified, unified, and reconciled unto himself, is instead the *open*, the multiple, a site of doubling and of paradox.⁶⁸ God does not produce sense; God does not organize and close off sense. Words such as "unity" presuppose or rather fetishize closure—they seek a system that echoes itself, that allows "once and for alls" to be announced from the Guild. Mainstream theologians may find offensive a God who is Open in the sense of radical openness, not only to the future but *as God*.⁶⁹ Of course, this is where we should suggest, alongside Nancy, Alain Badiou, and a many other postsecular philosophers and thinkers (or whatever we are calling us these days), that retiring the word "God" is a helpful move. But God haunts, as the open; God is still passing by.⁷⁰ A new materialist ontology, a new immanent metaphysics of openness, a new definition of the infinite as the finite: all these things still require the language we have inherited. It may be alright if Theo(s) comes back to haunt the cleared atheist ground, the new compound. It is not under threat. Not if God is queer, at any rate.

Nancy's wrestling with the inheritance of the incarnation is more nuanced than a simple rejection, but nevertheless remains deeply ambiguous. The very structure of the doctrine of incarnation preserves a dichotomy between God and world/flesh/bodies, a dichotomy that Nancy understands to be a source of Western imperialism, globalization, and dominance. In short, the incarnation plays a part in a worldview that Nancy passionately rejects, and indeed sees as dangerous and destructive. Rather than simply being opposed to the incarnation, however, Nancy finds traces within the doctrine that allow for its deconstruction from within. While the "spirit-body" of the Gospel of John leaves him cold, the a/theologizing of God in becoming flesh remains a site of production for Nancy, a place where the unraveling of Western hegemony can take place. To summarize all too briefly, the incarnation simultaneously reifies a God on High who deigns to enter this world from outside, and explodes such a God. The dichotomy breaks apart, not into a new monolithic structure of World alone (the world simply substituted for God), but rather into multiplicities. When God exits the scene, a new ontology becomes possible, one that reflects and even celebrates the spaces between us, the 'being singular plural' that constitutes not only our worldly experiences, but the fundamental being of the world.

Traditional Christologies, of course, would have none of this—and yet we find lurking in Christian doctrine exactly what Nancy says we will find: self-deconstruction. In the writings of the early patristics, there are moments of slippage as they struggle to hold together that which cannot be held: God-man. Likewise, in kenotic theology, the self-lowering of God as a body takes on systematic implications: the *kenosis* of God in Christ becomes the main metaphor or the fundamental clue into the nature of God, and this clue or metaphor reveals a God atheized (if we take such theology to its logical conclusion). Indeed, this is why it has been rejected by most mainstream theologians. It is in kenotic theology that we find intimations of an a/theology to come.

Finally, in current thinkers, those who for a variety of reasons find themselves to be somewhat marginal, we find a kenotic theology of the 21st century: Jesus not as the Other from on high, but the other despised *in* this world, as part of this world. The systems of Christianity undo themselves in the body of Christ. Rather than spirit, bodies—broken, isolated, hurting bodies—are the focus in both DiNovo and Keen. The incarnation makes this world the priority, in all its senses, so much so that God is transgressed, ruptured, and broken.

What does this mean for us? For Nancy? Dare I say that there is common ground? Probably not. The word "ground" itself is too loaded a term, and too solid and singular. Rather, let us say that the ground is being tilled, in multiple sites and by multiple thinkers who may not even agree that their projects echo each other. Nevertheless, I think they do. Theology from the margins has approached the incarnation with fresh eyes—and with eyes that the guild of theology may label heretical in their excesses. Such a heresy opens up the body of Christ in incarnation to a new Christological ethic, one that values the bodies that come to us *as* bodies, as sites of strangeness and exteriority. Even our own bodies approach us from outside—but it is an immanent outside, for both Nancy and for marginal theology. God becoming flesh, becoming a body in the world, requires a thinking that opens the world to itself, as itself, without need for an outside any longer. While Nancy would reject the retention of "God," the structures at play shadow and mirror each other. If Nancy is serious that the global hegemony the West has constructed must be undone, there are willing partners in that work from within the field that seems to be the most troublesome: theology itself.

NOTES

1. Jean-Luc Nancy, *Dis-Enclosure: The Deconstruction of Christianity*, 150.
2. See the Chalcedonian definition established in 451CE: ". . . we all with one voice confess our Lord Jesus Christ one and the same Son, the same perfect in Godhead, the same perfect in manhood, truly God and truly man, the same consisting of a reasonable soul and a body, of one substance (*homoousios*) with the Father as touching the Godhead, the same of one substance with us as touching the manhood, like us in all thing apart from sin . . ."
3. Both options were raised in the pre-doctrinal debates, and both were rejected.
4. See Ronald E. Heine versus Wolfhardt Pannenberg—the move to understand patristics as Scripturally grounded rather than philosophically oriented was undertaken only in the last 20 years.
5. See Daniele Rugo, *Jean-Luc Nancy and the Thinking of Otherness*, 36. B. C. Hutchens also insists that Nancy rejects incarnational thinking and this is true—if by incarnational thinking one means traditional classic Christian doctrine.
6. B. C. Hutchens, *Jean-Luc Nancy and the Future of Philosophy* (Montreal, Quebec: McGill Queens University Press, 2005), 86.
7. See Jean-Luc Nancy, *Noli Me Tangere*.
8. See Christopher Watkin, *Difficult Atheism: Post-Theological Thinking in Alain Badiou, Jean-Luc Nancy, and Quentin Meillassoux* (Edinburgh: Edinburgh University Press, 2011).
9. Jean-Luc Nancy, *Corpus*, trans. Richard A. Rand (New York: Fordham University Press, 2008), 65.
10. "In the beginning was the Word, and the Word was with God, and the Word was God. He was in the beginning with God. . . . And the Word became flesh and lives among us, and we have seen his glory . . .". John 1:1.
11. Nancy, *Corpus*, 65.
12. Ibid.
13. Ibid.
14. Ibid., 69.
15. While this articulation may resonate with some early theories regarding the incarnation, it is not sustained as such in Christian theology. The body does not need to be *merely* a site of signification and disembodiment within the Christian tradition and indeed, there are theologians who would shudder at the thought.
16. Ibid., 77.
17. "Sense" is a key term in Nancy's own corpus, and one that cannot be given its due here. After all, Nancy has devoted whole books to the subject (see *The Sense of the World*, *Being Singular Plural*, etc.). A gross oversimplification would be that transcendent sense—meaning or value given to the world from the outside, from something in excess of the world—is dead; this leaves us in a world without meaning—and yet this very condition, this absence of meaning, is itself a new kind of meaning, one that is provisional, tenuous, passing, rather than absolute, stable, and eternal. Nancy seek to avoid both a reification of absolute sense, and a nihilism that insists the world is devoid of meaning. If there is nothing beyond the world, then the world is all there is—and the world is constituted *as* bodies.
18. Nancy, *Corpus*, 25.
19. Ibid., 31.
20. Ibid., 61.
21. Ian James provides a helpful and succinct account of Nancy's concept of space: ". . . space, in this context, is not the three-dimensional extension as measured by geometry. Rather, in Nancy's terms, it is an exteriority, a spacing or *espacement*, which is at the same time also a temporalizing movement, an opening up of spatiality prior to space as we might traditionally think it." *The Fragmentary Demand: An Introduction to the Philosophy of Jean-Luc Nancy* (Redwood City, CA: Stanford University Press, 2005), 65. James presents Nancy's relationship to phenomenology in Husserl, Heidegger, and other German thinkers as his launching point for rethinking spatiality in these terms.
22. Ibid., 65, emphasis added. This is not a bad description of the contortions the early Church went through in attempting to articulate the relation of Father to Son in Jesus.

23. Nancy, *Corpus,* 126.
24. Ibid.
25. Ibid., 132.
26. Nancy, *Dis-Enclosure,* 73.
27. Ibid., 69.
28. Ibid., 70.
29. Ibid.
30. Ibid., 71.
31. Ibid., 82.
32. Ibid., 83.
33. Ibid., 115.
34. Ibid., 116.
35. Ibid., 61.
36. Ibid., 9.
37. "The Wonder of the Incarnation," *Crossroads Initiative,* accessed January 10, 2015, https://www.crossroadsinitiative.com/library_article/84/Wonder_of_the_Incarnation___St._Gregory_Nazianzen.html. Gregory's works are gathered in the five *Oratio,* and in the collected volumes of the *Patrologiae Gracae.* However, his words have been appropriated for worship and study by both the Roman Catholic and Eastern Orthodox churches.
38. Philippians 2:6-8.
39. Cyril of Alexandria, "On the Incarnation of the Only-Begotten," *Tertullian.org,* accessed January 10, 2015, http://www.tertullian.org/fathers/cyril_scholia_incarnation_01_text.htm.
40. "Nor is it divided, since it all exists alike; nor is it more here and less there, which would prevent it from holding together, but it is all full of being. So it is all continuous: for what is draws near to what is." Parmenides, "Fr. 8, 22-5, Simplicius in Phys. 144, 29," *The Pre-Socratic Philosophers,* ed. G.S. Kirk et al (Cambridge, UK: Cambridge University Press, 1983), 250-1.
41. This is stated by Pascal, Martin Buber, and others in various works over the course of centuries. In short, the onto-theological Being (unmoved mover, Eternal Good, etc.) found in ancient Greek philosophy and adopted into Christianity via neo-Platonism and Aquinas' use of Aristotle bears little resemblance to the God of Abraham, who experiences rage and forgiveness, changes his "mind," and cedes power to, for example, his Adversary (in the Book of Job). For an exceedingly analytical account of this claim, see (if you dare) Norbert Samuelson, "That the God of the Philosophers Is Not the God of Abraham, Isaac, and Jacob," *Harvard Theological Review* (1972): 1-27.
42. Heine, *Classical Christian Doctrine,* 84.
43. Cyril, "Commentary on the Gospel of John 1:14," *Tertullian.org,* accessed January 11, 2015, http://www.tertullian.org/fathers/index.htm#Cyril_Commentary_on_the_Gospel_of_John
44. Philip Schaef, "Creeds of Christendom, with a History and Critical Notes, Vol.2," Christian Classics Ethereal Library, accessed January 11, 2015, http://www.ccel.org/ccel/schaff/creeds2. For a cogent analysis of what Chalcedon is and is not claiming, see Sarah Coakley's "What Does Chalcedon Solve and What Does It Not? Some Relfections on the Status and Meaning of the Chalcedonian 'Definition,'" in *The Incarnation,* ed. Stephen T. Davis et al (Oxford, UK: Oxford University Press, 2002).
45. Athanasius, *On the Incarnation,* trans. John Behr (Yonkers, NY: St. Vladimir's Seminary Press, 2012), 51. Emphasis added.
46. Ronald E. Heine, *Classical Christian Doctrine* (Grand Rapids, MI: Baker Academic Press, 2013), 86.
47. Justin the Martyr's thought provides the best example of the Christianizing of Plato. God is transcendent and hidden; Logos is the intermediary between God and the created order. Logos is produced by God much in the way that speech is produced by a human being—we lose nothing by 'creating' speech; speech (often) reflects our thoughts (reason); speech is external to us and affects others. Logos becomes the revelatory agent for God in the world,

culminating in the Incarnation, "when the Logos took flesh in the Virgin, was born, and lived among us." Heine, *Classical Christian Doctrine,* 43.

48. Origen, of course, was not reading Aristotle. However, other philosophers of the time period had categorical classification systems similar to Aristotle's, and thus the category of relation used by Origen in his argument is very close to Aristotle's. His known philosophical influences were Philo and Numenius of Apamea.

49. Origen was writing well before the establishment of the creeds, and much of his philosophy was later rejected by the 5th century church for its "demiurge" elements regarding the person of Christ.

50. "I believe in one God, the Father Almighty, Maker of heaven and earth, and of all things visible and invisible. And in one Lord Jesus Christ, the only-begotten Son of God, begotten of the Father *before all worlds*; God of God, Light of Light, very God of very God; *begotten, not made*, being of one substance with the Father, by whom all things were made." Schaef, "Commentary." Emphasis added.

51. See Chrysostom, "Homily VII: Philippians 2:5-11," *Christian Classics Ethereal Library,* accessed January 11, 2017, http://www.ccel.org/ccel/schaff/npnf113.iv.iii.viii.html. Kierkegaard spends much of the opening segments of *Practice in Christianity* poetically expressing Christ's invitation, and then extrapolating from there the necessity of Christ's kenotic act.

52. Wolfhardt Pannenberg, *Jesus: God and Man*, trans. Lewis L. Priebe et al (Philadelphia, PA: The Westminster Press, 1977), 310.

53. John Macquarrie, "The Pre-existence of Christ," *Expository Times* 77 (1966): 99.

54. Many scholars, Pannenberg included, see in the confession of Chalcedon a tendency to treat Christ's humanity as less important, or less "real," than His divinity. Docetism in the early Church understood that God only "appeared" to have a body as Jesus—that the Incarnation was essentially illusory.

55. Macquarrie, "The Pre-Existence," 201.

56. Craig Keen, *The Transgression of the Integrity of God: Essays and Addresses,* ed. Thomas J. Bridges and Nathan R. Kerr (Eugene, OR: Cascade Books Press 2012), 31. Again, we find *kenosis* as a central theme or concept.

57. Ibid., 7.

58. Ibid., 10.

59. Ibid., 12.

60. Ibid., 15.

61. Ibid., 20. Emphasis mine.

62. Ibid., 27.

63. I admit with shame that this is a definition from dictionary.com. http://www.dictionary.com/browse/queer.

64. Judith Butler, *Bodies That Matter* (New York: Routledge Press, 1993), 228.

65. Cheri DiNovo, *Que(e)rying Evangelism: Growing a Community from the Outside In* (Cleveland, OH: The Pilgrim Press, 2005), 61.

66. DiNovo, *Que(e)rying Evangelism,* 66. This last is where I find most theologians to be lacking in a more prior, more abysmal, understanding. The incarnation is under no obligation to make sense. Most modern theologians simply cannot/could not reconcile themselves to mystery-as-mystery, to God's attributes being, in the end, perhaps *wrong*.

67. Ibid.

68. What I find so sad about even Pannenberg's attempts at Christology is his deep dependence upon rationalism, not in the sense of a Cartesian philosophy but in the sense of the necessity that God make sense. God does not make sense—in both the everyday usage of that phrase and in the Nancean enunciation.

69. God is open not in the sense of Open Theism, which is another system perhaps ultimately enslaved to theoretical closure from a Nancean point of view.

70. Nancy, *Dis-Enclosure*, 120.

Chapter Two

Raising Up the Body of Christ

> What *anastasis* would designate...is nothing other than redress, this raising up...of ruined sense like a truth cast forth, appealed to, announced, and saluted. Truth cannot but be saluted, each time, and never saved...
> —Jean-Luc Nancy, *Dis-Enclosure*

For a reader familiar with Christianity and Christian doctrine, the shift from incarnation to resurrection may seem abrupt. Where, one may ask, is the crucifixion in Jean-Luc Nancy's work? It remains largely absent as a consistent, well-developed theme. *Death* pervades Nancy's work—it is assumed, explored, gestured toward, saluted—but the specific crucifixion of the specific body of a man from Nazareth who is later understood as the Son of God is not addressed. It may be that the crucifixion event is not crucial to Nancy's work because death is found *in* and *as* resurrection *(anastasis)*. Because Nancy refuses the Christian concept of transcendence or ascension, resurrection is not a miracle of *life*, but an infinite extension of *death*.[1] Aside from a few comments in *The Inoperative Community,* an earlier work, most of Nancy's comments regarding resurrection are found in *Dis-Enclosure: The Deconstruction of Christianity* and in *Noli Me Tangere*. By relying primarily upon Maurice Blanchot's writings in the former, Nancy distances himself from more direct contact with Christian scripture and doctrine regarding resurrection. (A notable exception is his preference for the Gospel of John, which contains the most detailed and robust stories regarding Christ's resurrection and ascension.) In *Noli Me Tangere*, Nancy focuses most upon the encounter between Jesus and Mary Magdalene—yet this is a book as much about painting and touch as it is about resurrection. He provides us with a narrow window through which to engage broader Christian theology on this subject, and, unlike his work on incarnation, there is not a clear line of development or nuance.

With resurrection, Nancy continues his project of de-theologizing Christianity. The resurrection in Nancy's works is not a miracle from the outside, but rather is death, resurrected. It is absence walking around, the self dissolved and yet...not. It is most certainly not about a new life, or resuscitation, and most certainly not about ascension. Even when Nancy uses the word 'transfigure,' we must both hear the echo from Scripture and resist an easy equation with it. Yet the words he chooses, and the angles he takes, regarding resurrection do correlate and echo Christian theology. In order to uncover those echoes, I explore both the early Church writings and current theological accounts of resurrection, particularly feminist theology and theological phenomenology.

A point of note: a challenge for those who remain firmly *outside* the Christian tradition is first to recognize that resurrection is not just 'one thing' in Scripture. There are two kinds of individual bodily resurrection depicted in the Gospels, and they differ qualitatively from each other. First, there is the resurrection of Lazarus, and of Jairus's daughter, both of which operate as temporary resuscitation. They are brought back to life, to *this* life, to the same life, the same flesh, and all will die (again). But Jesus's resurrection is different from all previous resurrections. Jesus does not die again, but ascends to the Father. Jesus has powers and abilities that Lazarus seemed to lack (the ability to traverse long distances in an instant, and walk through walls, for instance). Lazarus and the young girl are both witnessed coming back to life by many; but the only *immediate* experience of Jesus post-resurrection is in John (not coincidentally Nancy's preferred Gospel), and it is *Mary's* experience alone.[2] Furthermore, Jesus's body is transformed, not just brought back to life. His body disappears (the wrapping cloths left behind), and then *something,* a body both the same and radically different, reappears. The church may call this body Jesus' *glorified* body, but nevertheless (as Craig Keen points out) it remains a mutilated body, a wounded body. Ascension did not *heal* or even completely *transfigure* Jesus's body. Additionally, different New Testament writers emphasize different aspects or even 'kinds' of resurrection: The Gospel of Luke lays heavy weight upon the physicality of Jesus's resurrection, while Paul (writing much earlier) indicates that "Jesus...has permanently left his home in the body," and that the resurrection "necessarily implied rising to a new kind of life."[3]

A third kind of resurrection also occurs in Scripture, one that is non-specific to any particular individual. It is the hope of the general resurrection of the dead, a hope found in post-exilic Judaism prior to the arrival of Christianity, particularly in Isaiah, Daniel, and in the apocryphal books of Enoch. This is in part a fuller articulation of life after death, a belief that did not exist in pre-exilic Judaism, but roared onto the stage once the exilic Jewish people encountered Zorastrianism in Babylon (a religion that has both a dualistic structure and a belief in the afterlife). Justice now extended beyond the flesh and the now, into life after death, and thus the resurrection of the dead was a necessary part of eternal justice, exacted upon everyone. There is differentiation among the prophets regarding what people groups are resurrected (only Jewish people? Everyone? Only the just?), but in any or every case, there is a hope that, beyond death, there will be justice.[4]

Paul opens the door to this application of Jesus's particular resurrection to the general resurrection in 1 Corinthians 15:

> Now if Christ is proclaimed as raised from the dead, how can some of you say there is no resurrection of the dead? If there is no resurrection of the dead, then Christ has not been raised; and if Christ has not been raised, then our proclamation has been in vain and your faith has been in vain. We are even found to be misrepresenting God, because we testified of God that he raised Christ—whom he did not raise if it is true that the dead are not raised. For if the dead are not raised, then Christ has not been raised. If Christ has not been raised, your faith is futile and you are still in your sins.

Jesus is the "firstborn of the dead," and the general resurrection of the dead follows theologically, as Christians are born again into life with Christ, and share in both his death and his resurrection.

A challenge for those who remain *within* the Christian tradition is to avoid making Nancy's project a straw man—a secular bugbear that simply does not properly understand Christianity. While Nancy's work on Christianity remains vulnerable to critique, it is not the case that he simply does not know his stuff; rather, his own acts of cherry-picking, or radical re-interpretation, echo the very history of Christianity itself, which throughout the course of its theological history has reimaged, reinterpreted, and repositioned key elements of the faith into new constellations. That the resurrection is not just 'one thing' is a lesson that those of the faith may need to remember as well. The topic of resurrection is extraordinarily complex—the New Testament writers have differing accounts and interpretations, and these are expanded upon in Christian thought throughout the centuries. To treat the resurrection of Jesus as a simple, naïve myth, as a skeptic *or* as a believer, is to fail to acknowledge the intricately woven strands of philosophy, religion, fear, hope, and dread that permeate Christian texts.

As is to be expected, the Early Church Fathers (Irenaeus through Augustine) wrote a great deal about the resurrection of the dead (also known as the general resurrection), and by default, address the resurrection of Christ. The resurrection of Christ is taken as a matter of faith, but also figures in defensive response to those thinkers, later grouped loosely into the category Gnostics, who argued for a less literal resurrection of Jesus. Some advocates of Gnosticism, (and later, the Manicheans), disparaged the flesh as the site of sin and death, and thus argued that the resurrection of Christ was spiritual, not material.[5] Gnosticism in particular seemed a reasonable route for Christian thought: it married the teachings of the Church to a Hellenistic mythic edifice, seeking to create a coherent and consistent articulation of both faith and a Greek worldview. However, faced with what many could call superior structural arguments, the Church—via councils, creeds, and condemnations—doubled down on inconsistent rhetoric that insisted upon both the real incarnation, death, and resurrection of Jesus in the flesh, and the real salvation of human flesh via the general resurrection of the dead.[6]

I follow a slightly different path in this chapter. First, I provide a summation of key teachings and writings of the early church regarding both the resurrection of Christ and the general resurrection. The aim is to provide a historical backdrop for Nancy's writings on the same topic, finding points of convergence or at least inspiration, thus demonstrating that Nancy is indeed conducting a deconstruction of Christianity, that the seeds of this deconstruction are present in the early church. Pulling from *Dis-Enclosure, Corpus,* and *Noli Me Tangere*, I trace Christological elements through Nancy's work. Understanding what he is reacting to remains helpful, particularly for those unfamiliar with a deeper history of Christianity. I then engage Nancy's work directly, returning only briefly to the early church in examining *Noli Me Tangere*. Finally, I attempt to build bridges by presenting how the resurrection is conceived and imagined by current theologians.

THE EARLY CHURCH AND THE RESURRECTION

While the incarnation as a matter of faith certainly presents obstacles enough for both Christian doctrine and the rest of the world, the claim that Jesus of Nazareth was "resurrected from the dead, ascended into heaven, and sits at the right hand of the Father Almighty"[7] presents far greater philosophical and scientific hurdles for theology and faith. Jesus's resurrection was unexpected even during his own era—the disciples expected Rome to be defeated, not their leader to die.[8] Nevertheless, an individual, rather than general, resurrection was a difficult pill for most first-century Jewish people to swallow, and it was truly madness to the pagan Gentile community surrounding them. At no point did Jewish messianism carry with it the notion of the messiah dying and coming back to life. All earlier metaphorical references to resurrection (Ezekiel, Daniel, Isaiah) pointed to a general resurrection of Israel, not to a single individual.[9] And even the aforementioned stories of resurrection found in Scripture (Lazarus, Jairus' daughter, etc.) were not true resurrection stories.[10] Such individuals were indeed brought back to life, but only to die again later. Their bodies were not glorified or changed; they did not gain the power to walk through walls or appear and disappear at will; and none of them ascended to heaven. Therefore, while first-century Judea was certainly boiling over with messianic hopes, and the notion of the resurrection of the body was taught by the Pharisees, the particularities of Jesus's resurrection do not seem to have a strong historical precedent.

Paul remains our earliest Christian source for any discussion of Jesus's resurrection.[11] He was not present for Jesus' resurrection (nor was anyone else for that matter) and only heard of it second-hand. His depiction and interpretation of Jesus's resurrection is framed through his encounter with Jesus on the road to Damascus—a spiritual, rather than physical, appearance that blinded him, and led him to convert:

> For I passed on to you *as of first importance* what I also received, that Christ died for our sins according to the scriptures, and that he was buried, and that he was raised up on the third day according to the scriptures, and that he appeared to Cephas, then to the twelve, then he appeared to more than five hundred brothers at once, the majority of whom remain until now, but some have fallen asleep. Then he appeared to James, then to all the apostles, and last of all, as it were to one born at the wrong time, he appeared also to me.[12]

The Acts of the Apostles (80–90 CE) gives us a sense of the confusion of the community during the decades following Jesus's resurrection and ascension. In the Gospels, two categories of post-resurrection accounts in the Gospels emerge: 'empty tomb' stories, and 'encounters with the risen Christ' stories.[13] Only in the Gospel of John is Jesus himself initially present at the tomb; all other versions of the tomb narrative have an angel or angels announcing the resurrection of Christ.[14] In the appearance narratives, on the other hand, the risen Christ appears to his disciples, who are hiding in fear, running away, despairing for the future, etc. From these scriptural elements, an elaborate faith in both the literal resurrection of Jesus, and in the general resurrection of the flesh of the dead, was born.

Key elements are present in all early church writings on the resurrection of Christ, but the most important conclusion was that this resurrection was 'in the flesh.' Rather than a mass hallucination, or an ecstatic vision, all the senses seem to be involved in these appearances. Christ, while risen, alive, and seemingly with some impressive powers of disappearance, reappearance, and unrecognizability, nevertheless still bears his wounds—the scars are visible. He eats (in the Gospel of John, he even cooks!). Augustine writes in a sermon on Easter, "But he rose from the sepulcher; and though his wounds were healed the scars remained. For this he judged expedient for his disciples: that he should keep his scars to heal the wounds of their soul. What wounds are these? The Wounds of their unbelief."[15] Earlier, Origen writes that Jesus's "whole person [was] covered with the marks of his valor."[16] Justin Martyr asks, "Why did he rise in the flesh in which he suffered, unless to show the resurrection of the flesh? And wishing to confirm this, when his disciples did not know whether to believe he had truly risen in the body...he let them handle him, and showed them the prints of the nails in his hands."[17]

In every case, the early church interpreted the body of Christ as that which bears the sins of the world, undertakes and glorifies the flesh created originally by God (which is therefore "precious" as Justin Martyr puts it in "On the Resurrection"), and overcomes Death itself in resurrection.[18]

With this interpretation of Christ's body as a given, the early church fathers spent most of their time defending, articulating, pontificating, and getting creative metaphorically with the general resurrection of the dead. Paul provides the church the first metaphor for general resurrection, using the seed/plant analogy to describe the resurrection of the body for believers:

> So it is with the resurrection of the dead. What is sown is perishable, what is raised is imperishable. It is sown in dishonor, it is raised in glory. It is sown in weakness, it is raised in power. It is sown a physical body, it is raised a spiritual body. If there is a physical body, there is also a spiritual body.[19]

However, this analogy is quickly discarded by the church as too organic and immanent.[20] It raised the problem of identity—the wheat grain in no way resembles the stalk, and there was deep concern that the 'selfhood' of each person be preserved in the resurrection. Secondly, it failed to account for all the sundry details required for dead, dismembered, disintegrated bodies to be made to stand again. Christ's body, after all, only lay in state for three days. Its wounds, while grievous, were not dismembering. As any number of crucifixes can attest, there is even a symmetry to the wounds, a melancholy gaping. Yet the early church insisted that in the general resurrection, such imperfections would be healed—that the new bodies given us upon the resurrection will be immortal, impenetrable, healed, made beautiful, without defect, and changeless. So even as Christ is the first resurrected body, his body, by its very wounds, differs from the bodies of the dead who will be resurrected. He is wounded; we will be made whole. Caroline Bynum interprets this as both an answer to the problem of Christ's delayed return (what about the saints' bodies that are decayed, already dust?) and as a balm to fears of putrefaction and decay.[21] In any case, however, and in whatever form resurrected bodies may have, the church has consistently held to the resurrection and salvation of the flesh, not just the soul. In spite of later Protestant movements that emphasize the Rapture or the destruction of the created world, for two thousand years the main bodies of the church have held to the goodness of material creation, and to the salvation of that material creation rather than merely an updraft of ghostly souls into some immaterial afterlife.

As already mentioned, the *identity* of the person raised was a matter of deep concern for the early church. One's body or flesh *was* one's self; therefore, when it is raised, it must be truly *you*, *all* of you. Early church writers were obsessed with both being eaten by animals (understandable given Roman ideas of entertainment at the time) and with cannibalism (also understandable, in that the early church was accused of cannibalism due to the language regarding eating the body and blood of Jesus in the Eucharistic liturgies). A body dismembered was a real fear for the early church, for how will God save a body consumed by a lion or fish, or another human being? If one's flesh has been absorbed by another's flesh, how can God reconstruct that person? Most thinkers—Irenaeus, Tertullian, Felix—insisted that resurrection was bodily restoration, that "all reality is corporeal."[22] Both Irenaeus and Tertullian held to an "extravagantly materialist notion of the resurrected body and an emphasis on radical change," evidently not being convinced that change equals a different identity.[23] Tertullian writes, "to be changed is to exist in a different form."[24] Therefore, just as Christ's body was glorified yet the same, and was truly *him,* so too will our bodies, when resurrected, be changed and yet *still us.*

If we wish to preserve identity and address decay, an inorganic metaphor must be used, and most church fathers preferred that of a statue that has been destroyed, gathered up, and remade by its creator. Resurrection becomes a re-assemblage of parts, even down to the atom, and with all parts present and made impassable, one's identity and salvation are enshrined for all eternity. It is not until John Scotus that we get something radically different. He argued that Christ was raised without biological sex and that "we are a self that flowers into an other that is inherent in the original pattern," reviving an organic metaphor but then applying it to a spiritual, not corporeal, body.[25]

Sarah Coakley also provides us with some insight into the early church understanding of body/soul, which then helps us understand the obsession with resurrection. She writes that in the early church, *sarx* or flesh indicated "total humanity, separated from God in sin," and that *pneuma* indicated "human personhood, when in obedience to God."[26] Thus, the difference between *sarx* and *pneuma* was not a matter of *kind* but of *relationship.* The human person is *sarx-pneuma*; each side of the hyphen gestures toward a different *relationship* with God. Paul, in his writings, does not use the *soma/psyche* division, but *sarx/pneuma.* Paul also seems to understand that the mind can be carnal (aka sinful—I can sin 'in thought'); therefore, the more simplistic "*sarx*=body, *pneuma*=soul" dichotomy doesn't follow from a careful reading of Scripture.[27]

What we find in the early church is a notion of body as identical as 'self': the body *is* the self, and therefore if salvation is real, the resurrection of the body is *necessary.* The 'ghost in the machine' notion of soul develops later. The rigid dualism that we assume is part of Christian doctrine does not exist, in fact, in early church writings. Even when the notion of the immortal soul starts to develop more fully, it nevertheless is inextricably linked to the body, such that the soul is unhappy and incomplete until reunited with the body. This is dualistic, of course, but it is more a dualism of parts rather than of essential difference. The body is not a meat puppet, worn and then discarded by the immortal soul. Rather, a *person* is this soul-body.[28]

What can we conclude from this study of resurrection in the early church fathers? First, that the soul/body dichotomy is far more complex in the early church than we often admit. Rather than simply rejecting the body or finding it disgusting, the early church fathers saw it as a key element to the full human person; indeed, some saw it *as* the human person. The immortal soul takes precedence in a later development in Christianity, and is linked to the re-discovery of Aristotle and his appropriation by St. Thomas Aquinas. While the body is a site of fear for the early church, that fear is directed at what happens to the body in death rather than at the body *per se*. While some church fathers indeed see the body as the site of sin, as something to be denied and dominated, in all cases the resurrection of the body nevertheless plays a major role in Christian doctrine. When presented with opportunities to resolve the inconsistencies in thought, the church instead retains the mystery.

Thus, when Nancy writes on resurrection in his works deconstructing Christianity, he is dependent upon these early teachings for his formulations, even where he denies the doctrinal conclusions. The sheer fact that Christianity amplified, developed, and tenaciously clung to the resurrection of both Christ and all the dead is what enables Nancy to perform his own dissections and reconstructions upon the body and upon Christianity. While again, Nancy certainly does not hold to the resurrection of the body in a Christian sense—he finds it, I would claim, too other-worldly, too dependent upon the absent God—nevertheless, that the body is so privileged in Christian thought from the inception of Christianity is something worth recovering.

Nevertheless, the death of the subject, which Nancy welcomes, the early Church would find abhorrent. The fear of loss of identity in death, the visceral terror of digestion and fragmentation, permeate the writings of the early Church. The resurrection of which Nancy speaks, which sacrifices the subject for the rise of death itself, would have been anathema to the Church, and indeed, would likely be met with resistance today on many fronts.

The above study lays the groundwork for a more detailed comparison and creative analysis. The early church took resurrection deadly seriously: it was *the* claim that distinguished the church from other religions. Indeed, their eschatology, hope, and liturgies all depended upon both the literal resurrection of Jesus, and the hope of the general resurrection of the dead. It is not shocking that most of the church writings tend to focus on the latter, however—parsing out the where and whys of Jesus's resurrection lends itself to circularity fairly quickly, as all of the Gospels conclude very quickly after their rather terse resurrection narratives. Paul's own reflections upon his conversion experience also focus more upon what the resurrection of Christ meant for Christians, rather than upon the event itself. Certainly, there were doubters right from the start (read Celsus for a bracing argument, dripping with scorn, regarding Jesus' resurrection). Nevertheless, the early church held firm, and more importantly, focused its attention upon the resurrection of the *body*, of flesh. It is this key point that provides us a tangential line into Nancy's own writings on the subject. For Nancy, as well, the crucial element of re-surrection is the "standing up of the dead body."

ANASTASIS: RESURRECTION IN NANCY

What does Nancy do, exactly, with resurrection? He utilizes the motif of resurrection in several works, but in a non-transcendent sense. While his writings easily lend themselves to tracing incarnation, when it comes to the resurrection of the body, Nancy relies upon Maurice Blanchot more than upon Christian doctrine, and addresses resurrection only obliquely in *Corpus*. Nevertheless, the resurrection of the body haunts his work, particularly *Corpus*. We must keep in mind the timeline of his work as well—*Corpus* predates *Dis-Enclosure*, and Nancy's deconstruction of Christianity is not fully developed in the former work. There is a lingering negativity, a kneejerk rejection of Christian thought, in *Corpus* that Nancy mediates in his later writings.

Corpus

While Nancy does not talk at great length about resurrection per se, I read his work on the body, in *Corpus,* as work on resurrection, even when he never uses that term. When he claims that the body as such is not mass, not substance (the most perfect substance being the point, which has no extension), but "the infinite of the finite," the opening, or that "the body consists of being exposed," he undoes the typical spirit/body dichotomy, and instead directs our gaze to the body operating otherwise than our philosophical constructs have thus allowed.[29] This deconstruction of body/soul leads Nancy to examine death, and to trace the trope of resurrection not to new life elsewhere, but to death here, now. In "On the Soul," he labels *spirit* as 'mass,' a single point without extension: "…what isn't the body is mass, or substance in the sense of mass, without extension…We can just as well call this spirit itself…"[30] He argues that throughout the Western tradition, discourse about the soul is just really about "the body outside itself."[31] The body both senses and is sensed, and is sensed by itself as well as by others. It is a Mobius strip of inside/outside.[32] Nancy also emphasizes the singularity of the body: 'This one here" is the factual case. This is the mystery of incarnation: that this body self-touches, senses itself, and is aware of itself as existing.[33] The incarnation in general terms is a correlate to resurrection, in that the incarnated body is a body opened to, standing in, or standing up in death.

This notion of the body as the site of sense-making as well as the exposing of sense leads Nancy to use the Christian adjective 'glorious' to explore further what happens to this body-towards-death, in the section of *Corpus* titled "Glorious Body." The use of 'glorious' carries with a significant Christian echo, in that a version of this adjective—glorified—is used to describe the resurrected body of Christ; therefore, I read this section through the lens of resurrection. In "Glorious Body," Nancy emphasizes that "Bodies are the ex-position of God and there is no other." God, in the creation of the world, ex-poses himself *dead* like *the world of bodies*. (At this point, Nancy is not being Christological, but I'm taking a bit of dramatic license.) Prior to this passage, Nancy wrote that "the body of God was the body of man himself: man's flesh was the body God gave himself."[34] The deep fears Bynum points out that color the history of resurrection in the early Church are echoed here in Nancy: "On the one hand, the divine body rotting, putrified, petrified, the face of Medusa and Death---and on the other, *as the other side of the same death of God*, the divine body exposed, the first material extension of a world of bodies."[35] Putrefaction, rot, and disintegration were the deep fears haunting resurrection discourse in the early church. Bodies rotting, falling apart—this is the fear that must be assuaged in the resurrection. But Nancy is using incarnation language here to describe not *Jesus*, but the creation of the world. Body is brought into being by matter modifying itself (the clay, *limon*, being shaped). God dies in this creation, in some way, for Nancy. In becoming body, God becomes matter, which is by definition mortal, finite. By doing so, God sets into motion the world of bodies, the only world we have or are. God's body, then, is exposed to, vulnerable to, death and all that comes with it. This mirrors the early church understanding of Jesus's sacrifice: he dies, and in so dying, defeats death. He does not override death, or eliminate death. He becomes death. Nancy's writing on resurrection insists that death is not eliminated in Christ's resurrection—and the church agrees. The theologian Karl Barth insists (and we will hear more from him later), for instance, that death does not vanish via resurrection:

> Nevertheless, wherever that crystal-clear word 'resurrection' shall be heard and understood, a prior word must be heard and perceived: 'Death.' It must be seen that in the midst of life, even in blooming and healthy life, there is a yawning chasm, a deep pit that cannot be filled by any art or power of man.[36]

Nancy writes, "This is the way God's glory is shared: Death, the World."[37] The language of glorified body, for Nancy, *is* the language of resurrection, *and* the language of death. Jesus's incarnated body was not glorified—the *resurrected* body was. "The glorified body is either *a transfiguration of the extended body* or its very extension, its figuration in malleable clay." The world stands up (*ana-stasis*) in/as the death of God.

The next section in *Corpus* is titled "Incarnation." By using the 'glorified' to indicate the act of creation rather than Jesus's resurrected body, Nancy places the glorified dead body of God *prior* to incarnation. The glorified body is *one* version of "coming to presence, coming and going," but another version of coming to presence is incarnation. This echoes the beginning of the Gospel of John ("In the beginning was the Word, and the Word was with God, and the Word was God..."), which informs subsequent creeds and doctrines regarding the relationship between God and Christ. Always-already, prior to the historical incarnation, Christ is at the beginning of creation, and thus the 'glorified dead body of God' is in some way ever-present, in its absence, well before a child was born in Nazareth around 4 BCE. The death of God is not first and foremost the crucifixion in Nancy's scan of Christianity; rather, the act of creation itself, by which this monotheistic God separates world from God, is God's first act of death, and this death is not annihilated in resurrection, but amplified.

Nancy later describes the body (and thus also the body of God) as a wound, writing that:

> the spirit is the *body* of sense, or sense *in* body. Spirit is the organ of sense, or the *true body*, the transfigured body. Here, then, in the spirit of Christianity, meaning Christianity as a theology of the Holy Spirit, is entire whole: a religion of breath (already Judaic), of impalpable touch, a religion of the word, of proferring, of exhaling—a deleterious odor of the dead...a general pneumatology... The Son is the Body of the Spirit exhaling in the face of the Pater...this body has passed into its wounds.[38]

Creation is the incarnation/death of God in matter. Jesus's dead, resurrected body does not end death—this fundamental leap of faith required for Christians is rejected entirely by Nancy. But Jesus's dead, resurrected body does echo, amplify, resonate, or concentrate that act of creation. That a singular, human body bears the weight of the incarnation of God—this radical move by Christian thought opens up the closed cosmology of the ancient world, and replaces the heavenly firmament above with empty space, the 'non-spacing of sense' from nowhere.

In Nancy's tracing, then, one discovers a strange crystallization. Christianity sowed the seeds of the death/absence of God via incarnation and resurrection, and one is able to see the fault lines in the construct of Christianity. But the loss of a closed cosmology, the opening of empty space where gods once dwelt, unravels a shared, common sense of the world (a shared meta-narrative, if you will). If we are, as human beings, "organized" to *signify* as Nancy claims, then what has been lost in this a/theologized world is the 'body of sense'—the whole, compact, mass-like organization of a place for everything and everything in its place. There is nothing *but* place, now; we *are* place, space, spacing. The fiction that has comforted the West for millennia—of static objects staying put in this neutral space—is gone, and it hurts, and we crave signification and significance. But instead what we actually do, when we think we are signifying in our writing, is an "infinitely finite suspending of this organization, a fragile, fractal, exposition of its anatomy."[39] We are in mourning for our lost structures—but these structures were suspended over an abyss, which is also the glorified/dead/resurrected body of God.

It is no surprise, then that the one section where Nancy does use the word resurrection in *Corpus* refers to writing, which ties back to his work on Blanchot: "What the Mystery reveals, therefore, is *the body as revealed Mystery*, the absolute sign of self and the essence of sense, God withdrawn into flesh, flesh subjectivized to itself, which, finally, is called 'the resurrection,' in the full radiance of the Mystery."[40] Ultimately, *Corpus* slides on the edge of a more robust deconstruction of Christianity. It is not until the essays of *Dis-Enclosure* emerge that we find a fuller, although by no means exhaustive, account of resurrection.

Dis-Enclosure

Nancy's deconstruction of Christianity emerges more powerfully in *Dis-Enclosure*. Here, Nancy primarily addresses resurrection via Maurice Blanchot, particularly his surrealist story, "Thomas the Obscure." In this work, Blanchot depicts the 'resurrection' of Thomas: Thomas emerges from his grave, but not into life, not recognizable, not as the subject he once was. "He (Thomas) appeared at the narrow gate of his sepulcher, not risen but dead, and with the certainty of being snatched at once from death and from life….the only true Lazarus, whose very death was resurrected."[41] Nancy, reading a lot into these few phrases of Blanchot, strips away the life of the person into death in resurrection, and insists there is no retrieval of that person, personality, ego, subject, but rather that the non-person now walks in/as death. Death is made alive, via the annihilation of the subject.[42] The resurrection in question "does not escape death, nor recover from it."[43] Resurrection, Nancy reads via Blanchot, is actually an unworking, a worklessness, in that it undoes the individuality, the subjectivity, of the one brought forth. This plays upon the deep anxieties of the early church regarding the continuation of personal identity via resurrection, *opposing* death.

Nancy states that Thomas's kind of resurrection does not go through death and out the other side (into life) but rather "resuscitate[s] death itself" (89). As Tenzan Eaghll has observed:

> The recognition of the death in life—the decline in the summit—is the gospel proclaimed by Christianity. However, according to Bataille and Nancy, the death of God in the Christian tradition signals the beyond within life, not the beyond that is beyond the world. The death of Christ makes death the very

resource of the divine other and thereby upsets the hierarchical distinction between high and low, father and son, good and evil.[44]

Nancy's resuscitation is not life anew, but death forever, and as such the resurrection is not a miracle but an unraveling of the subject and the infinite continuation of death itself.

Likewise, in the all-too-brief "Consolation, Desolation," Nancy describes *anastasis* as "not coming back, lying dead, he stands aright, stands anew in a saluted truth," a truth that cannot be "saved, for there is nothing to save, nothing to carry back up from the depths of the death: yet even that *is saluted*, hailed, each time..."[45] Nancy claims to be reworking resurrection so as to "turn around its value." Rather than pointing to resurrection as a source for hope of rescue from outside the world, or at the end of the world, Nancy sees resurrection as an act performed, in a sense, by the living to the dead, and from the dead to the living. A gesture, an acknowledgement of what has passed and will continue to pass.

But is *Jesus's* resurrection a recovery from death, an escape from death, even in Christian doctrine? Nancy claims that the state of resurrection described in "Thomas the Obscure" echoes in some way the "manner of advancing peculiar to the Resurrected par excellence."[46] The story of Thomas is the story of *the* resurrection, "following the example of Christ."[47] Thomas himself observes the resurrection of Anne, who imposes herself "upon the senses" in a bodily way. Thus, resurrection, in Nancy's reading of Blanchot, "designates access to that which is beyond *sense*" and here we need to hear echoes of Nancy's earlier use of that word.[48] There is a space that is nonspace, from which all sense emerges but which itself is sense-less, empty, abysmal. "The space of the resurrection...is the space outside of sense that precedes sense and follows it."[49] Nancy returns to the annihilation of subjectivity as a part of this resurrection of death itself—death does not happen to *me*, but rather is the "common and anonymous fate" of everything, every one: "Death resurrected, absenting me from myself and from sense, exposing me not only to the truth but exposing me at least as myself the truth."[50] Thus, if we understand Jesus's resurrection as a "ponderous return to life," like Lazarus's,' then indeed resurrection is a comforting, childish fiction created by religion to stupefy the masses. But Nancy seems to suggest that "death resurrected" is not focused upon the substance, the ponderous nature of death. Rather, the experience of death resurrected is that of experiencing the heavy *as* the light, infinitely—of all sense 'lightening' or lifting.[51] As such, it seems that the Resurrected one's own resurrection may not be a plodding zombification, but rather something we can turn around and read as a salute to absence.

Nancy and Blanchot also resort to metaphors of music and dancing in their attempts to describe an immanent resurrection and concomitant death of the subject. Nancy writes, "This song only sings, or this step only dances, at the moment of its breaking off, in the breaking of its breaking off, and it cannot do otherwise than *entrust to its own dying the task of sustaining its note, of dancing its step*."[52] There is an intimation of trust, as well as a caesura, a cessation of happening, an in-breaking. The dance may only continue *as* it ends. The text is entrusted—there is no return, no preservation, only a stopping, with acceptance.

And what could resurrection be in doctrinal Christian faith, other than a stopping and a trusting? Nancy writes that "resurrection ... erects dying, like the thick, and heavy gravestone ... to be ultimately obliterated"—the writing fades, the stone is worn away.[53] And again, "the consent to resurrection consents primarily to the *refusal* of belief, just as faith denies and rules out that same belief." Nancy concludes, "philosophical onto-theology practices embalming, or the escape of the soul—but never resurrection."[54] Once again, we come full circle: While doctrinal Christian thought may read the resurrection as a return to life (and we have already seen that this is a simplistic reading that does not account for the manifold interpretations of the resurrection found in the New Testament itself), it also unravels philosophical onto-theology from within via its impossible claims. The theology of resurrection via Paul, and the early Church, is a much weirder thing than it is given credit for. Rather than a "ponderous return to life," there are new *bodies, spiritual* bodies, bodies that are still material, bodies that are now imperishable; bodies that seem to defy every part of the definition of "body" and yet still remain body and not simply spirit.

Succinctly, then, Nancy uses Christianity to rescue thought *from* Christianity. Using Christian tropes, he pushes against the otherworldly tendencies within Christian doctrine. He ties the resurrected body firmly to the earth, but also insists on its multiplicity. Rather than a single gate through which salvation comes, Nancy's resurrected body is every body. But Christianity shares this *partage*, this expansion of resurrection and this rejection of the merely spiritual.[55] Surely, Christian dogma and practice has in many ways entombed and embalmed the body of Christ, enshrined it and made it inaccessible.[56] But this is not Christianity *per se,* or at least not the only Christianity. Christianity, in its weird doctrines, can undo the monolithic tendencies it carries with itself. While Christianity retains an inside/outside dichotomy that Nancy finds untenable, perhaps its own auto-deconstruction saves it from mere onto-theology.

Noli Me Tangere

The final place we encounter the resurrected Christ in Nancy's work is in *Noli Me Tangere*, a quick yet careful study of Renaissance paintings depicting the encounter between Jesus and Mary Magdalene at the empty tomb.

The 'origin story' from John reads as follows (I have excerpted the Mary Magdalene account):

> Early on the first day of the week, while it was still dark, Mary Magdalene came to the tomb and saw that the stone had been removed from the tomb... But Mary stood weeping outside the tomb. As she wept, she bent over to look into the tomb; and she saw two angels in white, sitting where the body of Jesus had been lying, one at the head and the other at the feet. They said to her, "Woman, why are you weeping?" She said to them, "They have taken away my Lord, and I do not know where they have laid him." When she had said this, she turned around and saw Jesus standing there, but she did not know that it was Jesus. Jesus said to her, "Woman, why are you weeping? Whom are you looking for?" Supposing him to be the gardener, she said to him, "Sir, if you have carried him away, tell me where you have laid him, and I will take him away." Jesus said to her, "Mary!" She turned and said to him in Hebrew, "Rabbouni!" (which means Teacher). Jesus said to her, "Do not hold on to me, because I have not yet ascended to the Father. But go to my brothers and say to them, 'I am ascending to my Father and your Father, to my God and your God.'" Mary Magdalene went and announced to the disciples, "I have seen the Lord", and she told them that he had said these things to her. [57]

Nancy's work here is ostensibly about painting and touch, yet the subject matter creates an opening onto larger questions regarding resurrection. Nancy reads this scene as that of revelation, but one must have "eyes to see." The condition for receiving the truth must be already present, already given. Jesus's appearance at the tomb in John is not the end of his *death*, like the end of a bad road trip. Rather, "the empty tomb un-limits death . . . he dies indefinitely. He is always departing."[58] Thus, the resurrection is the "discontinuity of another life *in* or *of* death."[59] Likewise, trust in our own resurrection is a stance of trust, not of belief. We, too, stand before death, and Jesus's stance before or, rather, after death does not discard or eliminate death from the scene.

Jesus is "the same without being the same" in his encounter with Mary at the tomb, Nancy claims. This echoes many of the Church Fathers on the subject, particularly Augustine. A brief foray through the few references made regarding this story in the early Church writings will help us to better engage Nancy's own slant. Some early Church Fathers interpreted his words as a direct response to Mary's mentality—that she was still relating to Jesus as she did before, but he had changed. Chrysostom writes, "Methinks that she wished still to converse with him as before, and that in her joy she perceived nothing great in him, although he had become far more excellent in the flesh." Jesus was claiming that "matters are not in the same state, nor shall I henceforth be with you in the same way."[60]

Origen also addresses this passage, and concludes that Jesus has not yet been purified from his "battle" with death, and is therefore ritually unclean!

Jesus needs to "wash his robe in wine" before being touched. Origen locates Jesus's great "baptism" not in his passion—that is, in his suffering and crucifixion—but in his resurrection through death. He was "on his way up to the husbandman of the true vine, the Father, so that having washed there and after having gone up on high, he might lead captivity captive and come down bearing manifold gifts—the tongues, as of fire . . . and the holy angels. For before these economies they were not yet cleansed."[61] Origen also asserts that Mary caught Jesus "in the act" of resurrection—that he needed to ascend to the Father before he could be touched; that purification of ascent needed to happen first. Nancy's focus upon the untouchable-touching of the bodies of Mary and Jesus seem to participate in this abeyance, this freezing of the frame.

Augustine likewise wrestles with why Mary is shut down from touching, while in the appearance narratives Jesus invites and cajoles people to touch him, even Mary herself (in Matthew). Augustine almost bails on the question, writing "It remains, therefore, that some sacred mystery must lie concealed in these words," but then makes a bold interpretation: Mary here represents the "Church of the Gentiles," who did not come to believe in Christ until he had ascended. It was not so much that she could not touch him, but that she had to touch him *in the understanding* that he was God: "Believe not thus on me according to your present notions; let not your thoughts stretch outwards to what I have been made in your behalf." "When you believe me to be God"—then you may touch me, is how Augustine interprets this scene. Likewise, Gentiles could not come to "touch" Christ without believing that he was at one and the same time God.[62] Augustine reiterates this in *Sermon 93*: "Whence He saith to the woman who represents the Church, when she fell at His Feet after His Resurrection, 'Touch Me not, for I am not yet ascended to the Father.' Which expression is understood mystically, thus: 'Believe not in Me after a carnal manner by means of bodily contact; but thou shall believe after a spiritual manner; that is, with a spiritual faith shalt touch Me, when I shall have ascended to the Father.' For, 'blessed are they who do not see, and believe.'"[63]

In Nancy's reading, again, Jesus is "the same without being the same." Jesus is who he is—yet he is not, and as such, one cannot relate to him as one had before. "He is his own alteration and his own absence"—again, Jesus embodies his own changes, and his very presence is a reminder of his inevitable and thus ongoing departure.[64] A further echo of church teaching is Nancy's interpretation of the "don't touch me" more correctly in the Latin as "do not *wish* to touch me." Following Chrysostom's logic mentioned above, Mary does not yet recognize the alteration and absence, and Jesus warns her not to desire touching, holding, caressing, as perhaps went on before. But Nancy takes it further, suggesting that Mary's desire to "hold on" is what Jesus warns against—Jesus is reminding Mary that there is nothing to *hold onto*, nothing to retain, no stasis or ownership, only empty space.[65] Mary thus "gives herself up to a presence that is only a departing, to a glory that is only darkness, to a scent that is only coldness." This description of the glorified body of Christ echoes *Corpus*'s understanding of God-as-already-dead, God as absence, infinitely. Nancy concludes this section by noting that "resurrection reveals that there is nothing to show, nothing to make appear out of the tomb, no apparition, and no theophany or epiphany of a celestial glory."[66] There is no sense to be made.

Nancy's concern for bodies as singular multiples also haunts *Noli Me Tangere*'s scan on resurrection. Rather than a resurrection *en masse*, or a single resurrection incident that never repeats, Nancy suggests that "everyone resurrects, one by one and body by body. . . . The resurrection designates [names, calls] the singular of existence."[67] Here, too, we hear an echo of traditional Christian thought, particularly the early Church Fathers' desperate need for identity, singularity, to remain in resurrection. The fear, almost palpable when reading the early Church writings, is that one will not be known as oneself, that one's deeds, personhood, will be lost in some sort of massive resurrection. Of course, ancient fears of mixtures, touches and combinations play into this hope surely; and what they meant by "identity" is surely not exactly what we mean now. Nevertheless, the singularity of each body as *a* body, and also and at the same time as *multiple* is something we find in both the writings of the early Church and in Nancy. Yet at the same time, Nancy plays with this desire for subjectivity, for "body by body" does not guarantee "self by self" or "ego by ego." The fear of the loss of identity present in the early Church (and alive and well today) is in some ways *confirmed* by Nancy, because one's identity is simply not as important as we think it is.

In many ways, however, Nancy's study of this scene is more a study of faith than it is of resurrection. As Ashok Collins notes:

> Nancy plays on the gap between Mary's mistaken belief that she is seeing a gardener and the reality of the risen Christ, emphasizing that the sense of the encounter is precisely in this gap of absence, which is not an absence at all but rather the "ordinary" singular plural relation of co-appearance taking place between all bodies rather than in any privileged exchange between the mortal body of Mary and the glorified body of Jesus. . . . Within the absenting of Christ, Mary is invited not to make the impossible possible, but rather to simply hold firm to the sense of her own existence in contact with a world of other singularities.[68]

While he explores the role of touching in detail, time and again Nancy returns to the notion of faith, defining it as "seeing and hearing where there is nothing exceptional for the ordinary eye and ear," a point he makes in the introduction to the volume as well.[69] Again, Collins: "Nancy's saturated faith, understood as an extension of his broader thinking on a/theology, is not belief in a transcendent 'God' but rather is a stance towards existence in which finitude is delimited and revealed as the singular plural with; it is simply recognized as what it already is."[70]

Nancy's theme regarding resurrection in this particular volume is one that he echoes in his work on Blanchot: resurrection is not the solution to death (despite what the Church Fathers may think). Instead, death in Western thought functions more insidiously as the locale of the dismantlement of "presence and absence, of animate and inanimate, of body and soul."[71] Interestingly, while the Church Fathers most certainly did see Jesus's resurrection, and the hope of general resurrection, as the defeat of death, they likewise saw it as the *dismantlement* of a body/soul dichotomy that de-privileges the body. Rather than siding with a clear, philosophically rational separation of spirit from flesh, as noted above, the early Church instead *insisted* that flesh in all its putrefying rot, decay, dismemberment and collapse is nevertheless gathered together and glorified. While certainly Nancy does not hold to this eschatological hope, nevertheless there is, in *Corpus* in particular, a hope *for hope*, or at the very least a mourning for the fragile, multiple bodies that pile up in our neoliberal world. Rather than embracing a coming Christian resurrection, Nancy faces death *as resurrection*—and radically interprets it as necessary for the spacing of bodies to exist in the first place.[72] Whereas traditional Christianity hopes for an end to death, Nancy finds his hope in death, for death "opens relation."

MODERN THEOLOGY AND THE RESURRECTION

There are myriad lines we may draw to separate paradigmatic and historical shifts in the history of Christian thought, and most of them could be challenged as arbitrary by at least one curmudgeon. For our purposes, rather than composing a thorough history of the minutiae of theological writings on resurrection over the past two thousand years, we turn to the nineteenth through twenty-first centuries as the time period most fruitful for comparisons to Nancy's own accounts of resurrection. One key element that distinguishes the early Church from this time period should go without saying: the advance of scientific discourse as the framing narrative for the Western worldview. As Paul Avis writes, "For the early Fathers, the mysteries and miracles of Scripture were paralleled and validated by the mysteries and miracles of nature . . . there was nothing so fantastic that early Christian intellectuals could not believe it."[73] While Irenaeus may not have known "where the birds go in winter," we undoubtedly do, and a lot more besides.

Furthermore, while the resurrection played a front-and-center role in the first three centuries of Christian thought, its centrality in Western theology dwindled and faded, while the crucifixion grew in scope and influence. By the time of St. Anselm, the emphasis was not so much upon the resurrection of the body of Christ but upon his atoning death. We are left with little material to work with.

Thus, the resurrection of Jesus Christ, while affirmed in the Apostle's Creed and other confessions of faith, remains a stumbling block for belief, just as it was in the first century. Modern concerns regarding resurrection mostly focus, however, upon whether it could truly have occurred historically. Theological explorations of this question range from the firmly materialist to the metaphorical/spiritualist. Most strict arguments for the resurrection make acceptance of it in some form a zero-sum game, absolutely required in order to be a "Christian," while works that attempt to engage it in a more worldly or skeptical manner end up projecting a rather blasé attitude with regard to its position as a critical matter for faith.[74] Indeed, the more liberal, and thus scientifically modern and palatable, view of the resurrection as a kind of special distinction for Jesus alone recommends that Christians should focus on having a spiritualized "God-with-us" now rather than any real hope for our own bodily resurrection. One can witness the latter approach in the works of Rudolf Bultmann, who, by embracing wholeheartedly Kant's limits to reason, rejects the resurrection as a historical event entirely and makes it a later mythological interpretation of a series of psychological events that happened to the apostles. By "solving" the dilemma of the historical resurrection, Bultmann erects in its stead a closed system—a system that cannot abide something radical or new breaking in upon it.[75] It is onto-theology, and for our purposes, it is insufficient. As Brian Robinette puts it, "rather than exploring the world of meaning that resurrection proposes for imaginative inhabitation . . . the resurrection of Jesus is typically treated according to the rather narrow concerns of traditional fundamental theology."[76]

But there would not be much of Christianity to deconstruct if it functioned perfectly as a closed system (and this is why criticisms of Christianity miss their mark when they simply equate it with onto-theology). While there is a plethora of recent theological literature about the resurrection, most of it falls into the dichotomy described above, and fails therefore to say anything *interesting*. What follows here is a patchwork, a cobbled-together exploration of a few key approaches to the resurrection in modern theology that manage to escape the question of historical possibility and instead focus upon the *meaning* of such an absurd doctrine.

Karl Barth

I begin with Karl Barth, the masterful Swiss theologian considered one of the best thinkers of the twentieth century. One of Barth's distinctive qualities as a pastor/theologian was his refusal to engage in abstract speculation about the nature of God. Rather, he insisted that everything we can know about the Judeo-Christian God, we only know via the actions and characteristics of Jesus himself. "No general idea of Godhead developed abstractly from such concepts must be allowed to intrude . . . [rather the definition of] Godhead is something which . . . we must always learn from Jesus Christ."[77]

Furthermore, Barth, while inheriting the typical "God as Being" language of his forefathers, nevertheless attempts to reinterpret such a claim by arguing that we may only discuss God-in-*action*—that to once again refer speculatively to the Being of God separate from his actions in Scripture is to head into dangerous waters. Thus, while Barth is well-known for his numbingly thorough (and unfinished) *Church Dogmatics*, and although he is certainly following on the heels of a lot of speculative theology, he works to maintain an implicit rejection of onto-theology in its most static, extreme form.

Barth writes:

> Before all created reality, before all being and becoming in time, before time itself, in the pre-temporal eternity of God, the eternal divine decision as such has as its object and content the existence of this one created being, the man Jesus of Nazareth, and the work of this man in His life and death, His humiliation and exaltation, His obedience and merit . . .[78]

Adam Eitel explains, "God's eternality should not be conflated with either intrinsic or extrinsic necessity; God's being is neither the 'mechanical outcome' of a 'process of rationality,' nor an 'event occurring through external causes.'"[79] Again, we find echoes of Nancy's own reworking of Christian doctrine in *Corpus,* emphasizing, if implicitly, the opening passages of the Gospel of John. This is the historicization of God's being, according to Barth, and it is easy to see how one can read this through a more secular, deconstructive lens (by bracketing "eternal," for instance) and tease out the notion of God's death (that is, his temporality) being sown/suggested/intimated at the very beginning of Christian doctrine regarding creation.

Regarding resurrection specifically, Barth understands the resurrection of Christ as a passive action upon him: "The facts themselves tell us decisively that the event of Easter has to be understood primarily as the raising *which happens to Jesus Christ*, and only secondarily and (actively) on that basis as His resurrection."[80] He also links resurrection to creation: "To raise the dead, to give life to the dead, is like the creative summoning into being of non-being, a matter wholly and exclusively for God alone, quite outside the sphere of any possible co-operating factors (Heb. 11:19; 2 Cor. 1:9; Rom 4:17)."[81] Eitel explains, "Barth frequently compares Jesus's resurrection to God's creation of the world. Barth sees in Jesus's resurrection an 'exact correspondence with what He did as Creator when He separated light from darkness and elected the creature to being."[82] Nancy's reading of resurrection via original creation, then, is not entirely radical or new—indeed it is the argument Paul makes in his second letter to the Corinthians:

> We always carry around in our body the death of Jesus, so that the life of Jesus may also be revealed in our body. For we who are alive are always being given over to death for Jesus's sake, so that his life may also be revealed in our mortal body. So then, death is at work in us, but life is at work in you. . . . Therefore, if anyone is in Christ, the new creation has come: [a] The old has gone, the new is here! [83]

While Nancy reads the creation of the world we now inhabit as the site of the death/resurrection of God, it takes very little imagination to read Paul's letter in a similar light. In the death/resurrection of Christ, a new world has launched, a world founded upon the absencing of God.

Bieler and Schottroff

In more current theology we may find some helpful resonances or at least some challenges to both liberal whitewashing and conservative inflexibility. In *The Eucharist: Bodies, Bread, and Resurrection*, Andrea Bieler and Luise Schottroff read the resurrection into Eucharistic practice and belief. They insist that "the New Testament traditions of resurrection are still burdened with dualistic misunderstandings," where the hope of the general resurrection is limited to the "future," rather than the present.[84] The death of Christ must be held together with his resurrection, in the remembrance of the Eucharist, such that participants are "members of Jesus's actual body . . . they themselves are risen."[85] Rejecting centuries of Christian argument regarding the regurgitation of body parts in the general resurrection, Bieler and Schottroff locate the resurrection of believers in the act of taking the Eucharist, and argue that the communion table is "where the resurrection is experienced."[86] This sounds very ecstatic and mystical without a lot of evidence indicating this to actually be the case. They argue that, "The Western passion for order, with its corresponding linear notion of time, is not content to trust the God of the living; it wants to know with certainty: have the ancestors been raised?" While Nancy would accept with grace this critique of Western monotheism, *and* would appreciate the rejection of "time" as the constitutive framework for analysis, nevertheless there is a lot lacking here—there are a lot of claims made, based upon Scriptural passages, but these claims are made as proclamations without development. It may certainly be a matter of and for faith that Christians should refocus their experience of the Eucharist toward resurrection, not merely crucifixion or the Last Supper, but a lot more needs to be said theologically about what this resurrected Body of Christ, now manifest in the Eucharistic offering, could *mean*, such that when I participate in said offering, I too receive resurrection.

Ultimately, Bieler and Schottroff's work is helpful from a political perspective: they take human bodies seriously, echoing some of Nancy's own concerns: "the bodies of human beings, created by God, were the objects of acquisitive political power; . . . of every form of violence that put human beings at the disposal of others."[87] By emphasizing the vulnerable, open, abused bodies that both litter and make up our world, and the equally vulnerable, exposed, martyred body of Jesus, and aligning said bodies with the body of Christ at the communion table, Bieler and Schottroff take a relatively radical step of requiring Christians to *address* their own bodies and the bodies of others in sacrament. We experience "physical communion" with Christ at the Eucharist—his body, our bodies, his body-as-our-bodies and vice versa. The loss of subjectivity this implies is never taken up by these theologians, of course, but the mingling of individualities, the rupture of boundaries between self and other, at least intimates a theological future for this line of thought.

Brian Robinette

Brian Robinette, professor of theology at Boston College, wrote *Grammars of Resurrection*, a masterful work that reads resurrection via the lens of phenomenology, particularly the work of Jean-Luc Marion. Rather than engaging in apologetics (rightly concluding that there has been plenty of work done recently that he has nothing further to contribute), he aims to engage the resurrection as "something [that] has therefore happened in and for our *world.* The resurrection of Jesus is an ontological reality. It concerns a *body*, and the body, from a Christian point of view, is not the impermanent shell for an immortal soul; it is just the way personhood is enacted in the world."[88] Relying heavily upon Marion's "saturated phenomenon," Robinette firmly locates the resurrection as precisely that: a *sui generis* event that "saturates' all perspectives."[89] The resurrection is a gift offered; our reception requires from us less an action than a "purgation," a letting-go of what keeps us from receiving the gift. He locates both ancient *and* modern skepticism regarding resurrection as stemming from "a sense of revulsion at an almost visceral level that I *am* my body," a position one can certainly justify by reading, for example, Gregory of Nyssa or any modern fashion magazine.[90]

For my purposes, some points of resonance between Robinette and Nancy beg for exploration. In particular, both thinkers (1) regard the body as multifarious and "plural"; (2) read the resurrection accounts as "absencing"; and (3) trace resurrection to both all of creation and to questions of justice (Nancy primarily does so in *Corpus). Grammars of Resurrection* is a massive text and well-worth the read, but I focus here primarily upon Robinette's reading of the resurrection accounts in John, and his own critique of Western thought, as his work with phenomenology, while interesting and important, does not intersect substantially with Nancy's more deconstructive approach.[91]

For early followers of Jesus, for the Church in subsequent years, and for modern science today, "the scandal of the empty tomb . . . is the *body*."[92] After all, Docetism was the earliest and most persistent heresy (aka, the notion that Jesus only *appeared* to be embodied). Robinette points out that modern believers are still uncomfortable linking the body to personal identity. We still think in terms of meat puppets despite our various fetishizations of the body in modern life. But the early church resisted both Docetism and other heresies that devalued the body, and instead insisted, and Robinette insists with them, that "the body is the very 'site' of salvation, and is so because God has assumed a body, a piece of creation, not just for a time, but for eternity."[93]

With Nancy, Robinette pushes against the Cartesian trend of separating self from body, and in so doing, both thinkers resurrect an earlier understanding of personhood as a "psychosomatic unity," rather than a duality. Relying upon Drew Leder's phenomenological work, Robinette reads the body as "a multivalent reality: ecstatic and recessive, visible and invisible, self-concealing and self-presenting."[94] This is a claim back to the psychosomatic unity we find in the early Church, but which also echoes Nancy's own writings in *Corpus*. Robinette links this weird experience, and this frustration with being driven by forces outside our control but within our own bodies, to Gregory of Nyssa's (and the other church fathers) deep disturbance over the functions of the body *and* to Heidegger's sense of "thrownness." But how does this inform a post-modern account of resurrection? Robinette argues that "this doctrine [of the resurrection] affirms that my self-identity is never unmediated, can never be seen as a monadic essence standing in disengaged relation to the Other; for through my body the Other is installed within me. . . . Bodies are relational and permeable."[95] Thus, "the affirmation of bodily resurrection is the affirmation of the relational self, the human being who comes into being corporeally as a being-with and a being-for."[96]

Similar to the arguments made by Craig Keen, Robinette argues that receiving the resurrection requires a dramatic shift in the way we act in the world regarding justice and mercy. He claims that the resurrection shows that God is the God of victims, and argues later that "belief in Jesus's resurrection issues a commission to live a life that involves potential danger since it involves bringing justice and reconciliation wherever personal and structural violence is found in the world."[97] Similar to Nancy's ethical call for justice regarding bodies, Robinette connects a robust understanding of self-as-body with an equally robust sense of ethics as being-with-others, profoundly and deeply connected while also existentially separate.

Robinette also addresses the resurrection accounts in the Gospel of John, particularly the *"noli me tangere"* scene that Nancy parses so well. Robinette understands Mary's experience as a "triple loss" in a way eerily reminiscent of Nancy's own description: "Only in *being recognized* was she capable of perceiving truly. Only in *being named* was she able to call out "rabbouni!". . . . Though fully 'present' to her in his transfigured corporeality, the risen Christ appears in the mode of 'absence.'"[98] Later he writes, "In John, the withdrawal of the physical body of Jesus from any objectifying view or grasp is the conditioning possibility for the presence of the risen Christ in the community." Robinette re-affirms many other readings of the Mary story: that she was trapped in a "pre-paschal imagination," still understanding and relating to Jesus as if he were as he was before. "The withdrawal of Jesus's body in resurrection and ascension, though very much an absence, 'announces the plenitude of God's presence' which communicates itself in and through a multitude of bodies . . ."[99]

Robinette locates this absence as an "excess" rather than an abyss, a plenitude and abundance rather than the ex-posure of the death of God. But at this point, and if justice and mercy and compassion are the "being-with" ethic driving both authors (which I think is true), one has to ask whether it *matters* that one sees a void and the other sees a saturation. It *does* matter, in that the saturation in question is an excess of Being, and that excess of Being falls back, or can fall back, into a static onto-theology. But surely such a collapse is not the inevitable product of excess.

Along with the focus upon excess rather than absence, Nancy would find the "fulfillment of history" eschatological language favored by Robinette a bit much, and this is precisely the point of divergence between faith and lack thereof. Robinette's work, and indeed perhaps theology in general, must assume (it seems) the outside/inside—the entering in of God from outside the world, thus making the world monolithic in its oneness. As Ashok Collins notes in his essay, "Toward a Saturated Faith," Jean-Luc Marion supposes an Other, an Alterity, a givenness that precedes intentionality. Nancy, on the other hand, accepts no such temporal or ontological primacy. "Givenness" is not quite his language. Rather, the co-appearances of beings-with are simultaneous with the making of sense and meaning. There is no "prior" to turn/return to. As such, Robinette's fundamental structure, which follows Marion in the embrace of an Other, betrays Nancy's project at its roots. Robinette writes, "the resurrection of Jesus from the dead remains Other to history, not as something alien or opposed to it, but as its im-possible Gift: as that which frees history from its own weight . . ."[100] Robinette's influences here are Derrida, Levinas, and Marion. While Nancy is somewhat sympathetic with Derrida, and is certainly open to the language of gift, the dichotomy this intimates evokes transcendence in a way that Nancy cannot bear.[101] However, it may be that Nancy emphasizes too much a notion of salvation *from* the world "rather than salvation *of* the world, history, and the body."[102] In Robinette's account, the resurrection undoes precisely the dichotomous structures that Nancy opposes in onto-theology: it "transgresses distinctions of subjective/objective . . . bodily/spiritual, historical/eternal . . ."[103] Jesus's resurrection is a "rupturing through the chasm of being and non-being"—a more-than-historical event.[104] Thus anything we say about the resurrection cannot simply be historical, but will "self-efface just as it declares, will unsay in the midst of its saying . . . as it makes present and near, it will do so while manifesting absence and distance."[105] Rather than embracing the hermeneutic of suspicion, Robinette claims a hermeneutic of hospitality, something that Nancy would both support and be wary of (for who knows what onto-theological dross one may let in the door).

Robinette's reliance upon the saturated phenomenon, with its resultant excess, is at odds with Nancy's more abysmal absencing.[106] Likewise, Robinette's understanding of the resurrection, presented in Paul and the Gospels and reconciled with the teachings of the early Church, requires a faith that exceeds Nancy's limits: After all, rather than death itself resurrected eternally, as Nancy argues, Robinette is well within orthodox boundaries by instead claiming that resurrection defeats death, even reverses it. So it remains a legitimate question as to what Nancy is up to regarding resurrection. Does this deconstruction work? Is there something really being read against the grain here, something uncovered, lurking in the heart of the resurrection? After all, deconstruction is not just interpretation; it is not simply an "anything does" philosophical "method." Rather, it is, at its best, an uncovering, a discovering, a reading-otherwise but within the frame of the given. I am not sure Nancy's reading of the resurrection meets this sort of criterion—which may be why he remains mostly within Blanchot's world rather than the strictly Christian writings and Scriptures. It is perhaps Nancy's work on resurrection that most clearly reveals the gulf between his writings and Christianity as a lived, and living, religion. While both the incarnation and, as we will see, the community provide deep and fruitful re-workings, the resurrection seems to stop Nancy short.

Nevertheless, something is recovered in Nancy's work that is key to Christian theology, and is often neglected, and it is what Robinette began with: the body as site of salvation. This body as site of salvation is not an atomized individual, but a corporeality that, from its very beginnings, has been multivarious, made of others, nurtured by another body in the womb, connected to another's circulatory and digestive systems (so writes Leder). My body comes first—prior to any sense of self that I then slough off as separate from my flesh. Modern Christianity, carrying forward the influence of Descartes and modern science, has lost this sense of bodiliness, and Nancy correctly diagnoses our Western disease in *Corpus*. Nevertheless, again it seems it is both onto-theology and modern scientific discourse that should bear the brunt of this mistake—and Christianity secondarily, of course, by making a world for Cartesianism and modern science possible. Nancy is right that Christianity, read against the grain, is *bodily*.

Craig Keen

Finally, once again we find that Craig Keen's work on resurrection resonates most closely, albeit still tangentially, with Nancy's. For Keen (and for many theologians), one cannot separate the incarnation from the crucifixion from the resurrection, and as such teasing out something systematic in his work regarding, specifically, resurrection necessarily involves talking about all those other terms, too. Nevertheless, both Keen and Nancy touch upon *kenosis* in their work, and we can trace this *kenosis* in Keen not just to and through the incarnation, but to and through the crucifixion and resurrection as well.

The *kenosis* of Christ, whereupon God the Absolute becomes a singular, frail, all-too-human body, extends to the resurrection of that self-same body. Now, this can unfortunately be read in a triumphalist tone, whereby by slight of hand God feigns death and escapes it via resurrection (and certainly early Christian thinkers, who were later branded heretics, suggested precisely that—for the notion that God would *die* was anathema to rational discourse). But this does not *require* a triumphalist reading, and this is where Keen threads the needle, maintaining (unlike Nancy) that the resurrection of Jesus Christ is indeed the death of death, the beginning of something new, while nevertheless holding fast not to some triumphant re-emergence of God from an infinitely thorough incognito, but to the radical idea that the body that is resurrected is still all-too-human, still wounded, still "kenotic." God remains broken, fragmented: "his stripes are not healed; he remains the lamb slain."[107]

Keen writes:

> Without the loss of his human nature or his human will, without the loss of his human heart or soul or mind or strength, without the loss of his human ignorance or weakness or vulnerability, that is, without the loss of his "flesh," Jesus becomes that human life which is the concrete movement of God into the world...*Here human being is opened to God and God is opened to human being.*[108]

As I have written elsewhere, for Keen, as for Nancy, the tomb is not just empty, but emptiness. Even the resurrection is empty—but this emptiness is *directed*. What is absent is not God *per se*, but what Nancy would read as onto-theology or monotheism.

Finally, both Keen and Nancy trace the body of Christ to creation. Nancy does so, as we have seen, in *Corpus*, finding the death of God not at the cross but at the beginning: in creation, God absents Godself and dies. Keen, along with just about every other theologian, reads Christ's death and resurrection as the dawn of new creation (taking this primarily from Paul's letters). Yet this new creation is not grounded in some universal stasis, nor in Being, but in the weak, tired body of a dead Jewish peasant, a dead Jewish peasant who nevertheless stands again, wounds still gaping, and grounds a new creation in, from a Western sensibility, nothing at all.

Nancy's deconstruction of resurrection is at times, or rather over time, contradictory, playful, morbid, and scornful. Resurrection rescued from a hope directed toward the outside, an afterlife, a place beyond, ends up being a resurrection of death itself, and this frustrates Nancy even as he wants us to face this. Nancy insists, having spent most of his adult life facing his own mortality directly in a way most of us have not, that the "only immortality possible is death," and that resurrection fools us when it "heals and glorifies death within death itself."[109] Yet facing death may yet be an act of faith, for "faith gives dying, in its incommensurability, a gift . . . that [one cannot] keep, any more than [one keeps] love," he writes in this same section.[110] The next chapter explores, among other things, Nancy's exploration of what a "faith in nothing at all" may do, and how the deconstruction of Christian faith may leave us with a way of being-with, a *doing* of being-with, that is not, strictly speaking, *hopeless.*

NOTES

1. It should be noted that death and resurrection are not separated in the Second Testament tradition either.

2. In Matthew, several women encounter Jesus away from the tomb. At the end of Mark, Jesus appears to Mary first, but these verses are disputed and are considered later additions.

3. Paul Badham, "The Meaning of the Resurrection of Jesus," *The Resurrection of Jesus Christ*, ed. Paul Avis (London, UK: Darton, Longman and Todd, 1993), 31.

4. One can hear Jacques Derrida's work on death prefigured here, in part. See his "Force of Law: The Mystical Foundation of Authority," in *Deconstruction and the Possibility of Justice*.

5. The Sethian School held to matter as being "servile," and trapped, whereas spirit was "immortal" and free from the "necessity of generation." See G. R. S. Mead, *Fragments of a Faith Forgotten: Some Short Sketches Among the Gnostics* (Whitefish, MT: Kessinger Publishing, 2005), 213. Some Gnostics return to the notion of the incarnation and argue that that, too, was spiritual rather than material. Parsing out the misrepresentations of Gnosticims within the early Church Fathers' writings is a work unto itself, but the Church interpreted their teachings to be dualistic and "libertine," in spite of evidence that some Gnostics were ascetics.

6. Post-enlightenment theology resurrects the debate via modern scientific discourse, and liberal theology tends to align itself more with a benign spirituality than anything approaching the radical impossibility of the resurrection of *sarx*, but that's a tale for another time.

7. "The Apostle's Creed," traditional version.

8. His resurrection confirmed the hopes of early 1st century Judaism, which already had a notion of the resurrection of the dead and of justice prevailing.

9. See Daniel 12:2; Isaiah 26:19; and some would say see Ezekiel 37:1-14.

10. See John 11:38-44; Matthew 9:18-26; Mark 5:21-43; 1 Kings 17:17-24.

11. Paul's first letter to the Corinthians probably dates to around 56 CE; the earliest Gospel (Mark) is dated around 80 CE.

12. 1 Cor 15:3-12.

13. See John E. Alsup, *The Post-Resurrection Appearance Stories of the Gospel Tradition* (Eugene, OR: Wipf and Stock, 2007).

14. The Gospel of John version is the one that Nancy seems to find more interesting, as it is the only account of the "Don't Touch Me" story, which is the basis of the paintings he deconstructs in *Noli Me Tangere*.

15. Augustine, "Sermon on Easter." *Catholicism.org*, accessed October 14, 2016, http://catholicism.org/st-augustine-easter.html ().

16. Origen, "Gospel of John, Book II," *New Advent*, accessed October 5, 2016, http://www.newadvent.org/fathers/101502.htm.

17. Justin Martyr, "On the Resurrection," *New Advent*, accessed October 3, 2016, http://www.newadvent.org/fathers/0131.htm.

18. Origen, "Gospel of John, Book II."

19. 1 Corinthians 15:42-44.

20. See Caroline Bynum's excellent book, *On the Resurrection of the Body*, for every metaphor used by theologians from 200-1336. To say its thorough is an understatement of significant magnitude.

21. Caroline Bynum, *On the Resurrection of the Body in Western Christianity, 200-1336* (New York: Columbia University Press, 1995), 108, 174, 221.

22. Ibid., 33, 35. This is interesting to place with Nancy in terms of a kind of immanence or denial of a world outside this world.

23. Ibid., 38.

24. *De Res,* Chapter 55, in Bynum, 36.

25. Bynum, 143. However, his thinking was not embraced by the Church. In fact, Pope Honorius III required that it be burned in 1210.

26. Sarah Coakley, *Religion and the Body* (Cambridge, UK: Cambridge University Press, 1997), 93.

27. Again, here we see echoes of Nancy's own work on this in *Corpus*.

28. This too is something we hear in Nancy, particularly in his essay "On the Soul." Rather than dismissing utterly the notion of "soul" as Gnostics dismissed the body, Nancy attempts to recraft what exactly "soul" is in relation to body, and in doing so he echoes some of the early church thinkers, with their psycho*soma*tic unity. See Michael Hanby, "Desire: Augustine Beyond Western Subjectivity," *Radical Orthodoxy,* ed. John Milbank et al (London, UK: Routledge, 1999) 109-126.

29. Jean-Luc Nancy, *Corpus,* trans. Richard A. Rand (New York: Fordham University Press, 2008), 123.

30. Ibid., 124.

31. Ibid., 126.

32. In this regard, he echoes Maurice Merleau-Ponty.

33. Ibid., 132.

34. Ibid., 61.

35. Ibid., 62-3.

36. Barth, Karl. "Threatened by Resurrection." *Bruderhof Communities.* Accessed November 1, 2016. http://web.archive.org/web/20030811093218/http://www.bruderhof.com/articles/Threatened.htm

37. Nancy, *Corpus,* 63.

38. Ibid., 77.

39. Ibid., 83.

40. Ibid., 87.

41. Maurice Blanchot, *Thomas the Obscure,* trans. Robert Lamberton (Barrytown, NY: Station Hill Press, 1988), 37.

42. This is directly against the hope of the resurrection expressed by the Church over the centuries. With rare exceptions, the Church was very interested in preserving identity between the dead body and the raised body, the dead self and the raised self.

43. See Kas Saghafi's "Thomas the Marvelous: Resurrection and Living-Death in Blanchot and Nancy," *Mosaic* 45/3 (September 2012), 1-16.
44. Tenzan Eaghll, "Jean-Luc Nancy on Sovereignty and the Retreat of the Christian God," *Res Publica. Revista de Historia de las Ideas Políticas*, Vol. 17 Núm. 2 (2014): 429.
45. Jean-Luc Nancy, *Dis-Enclosure: The Deconstruction of Christianity*, trans. Bettina Bergo et al, (New York: Fordham University Press, 2008), 101.
46. Ibid., 92, meaning Jesus' resurrection.
47. Ibid.
48. Ibid, 93.
49. Ibid, 94.
50. Ibid.
51. Ibid, 95.
52. Ibid, 96, emphasis mine.
53. Ibid.
54. Ibid., 97.
55. Nancy uses *partage* frequently, in the sense of "sharing out" or "sharing with."
56. I think here of the closed table of the Eucharist in Catholicism, and the refusal to ordain women in Orthodoxy, Catholicism, and many Protestant denominations. Such practices reserve the body of Christ, and such reservation is a kind of entombment.
57. John 20:1-18. Roy D. Kotansky writes, "Having a woman of questionable repute (a former demoniac), all alone among women, being described as actually embracing Jesus, postmortem, might have been too much for some scribes to fathom. Nevertheless, the Matthean narrative can be seen to capture the essence of a story that both John and Matthew must have acquired, independently, from a common source, probably an orally based eye-witness report." "The Resurrection of Jesus in Biblical Theology: From Early Appearances (1 Corinthians 15) to the 'Sindonology' of the Empty Tomb," *Reconsidering the Relationship between Biblical and Systematic Theology in the New Testament,* ed. Benjamin E. Reynolds, et al (Tubingen, Germany: Mohr Siebeck, 2014), 101.
58. Jean-Luc Nancy, *Noli Me Tangere*, 16.
59. Ibid., 17.
60. John Chrysostom, "Homilies on the Gospel of John, Homily 86," *New Advent*, accessed August 26, 2016, http://www.newadvent.org/fathers/2401.htm.
61. Origen, "Gospel of John, Book II."
62. Augustine, "Tractate CXXL," *New Advent,* accessed September 1, 2016, http://www.newadvent.org/fathers/1701121.htm.
63. Augustine, "Sermon 93," *New Advent*, accessed September 1, 2016, http://www.newadvent.org/fathers/160393.htm.
64. Nancy, *Noli Me Tangere,* 28.
65. Ibid., 37.
66. Ibid., 45.
67. Ibid., 47.
68. Ashok Collins, "Toward a Saturated Faith: Jean-Luc Marion and Jean-Luc Nancy on the Possibility of Belief After Deconstruction," *Sophia* vol. 54 (2015), 54: 336.
69. *Noli Me Tangere,* 22.
70. Collins, 338.
71. *Noli Me Tangere,* 44.
72. Ibid., 45.
73. Paul Avis, *The Resurrection of Jesus Christ* (London, UK: Darton, Longman, and Todd, 1993), 8.
74. See, for example,
75. Bultmann's use of the word "myth" in his work is complex. He relies upon Martin Heidegger's concept of demythologizing ancient traditions, writing "It is impossible to repristinate a past world picture by sheer resolve, especially a *mythical* world picture, now that all of our thinking is irrevocably formed by science. A blind acceptance of New Testament mythology would be simply arbitrariness; to make such acceptance a demand of faith would be to

reduce faith to a work." Rudolf Bultmann, *New Testament and Mythology and Other Basic Writings*, ed. Schubert M. Ogden (Philadelphia: Fortress, 1984), 3.

76. Brian Robinette, *Grammars of Resurrection: A Christian Theology of Presence and Absence* (Spring Valley, NY: The Crossroad Publishing Co., 2009), 17-8.

77. Karl Barth, *Church Dogmatics IV, Volume 1*, ed. G. W. Bromiley et al (Edinburgh: T & T Clark, 1957), 129.

78. *Church Dogmatics* II, *Volume 2*, 116.

79. Adam Eitel, "The Resurrection of Jesus Christ: Karl Barth and the Historicization of God's Being," *International Journal of Systematic Theology* 10: 1 (2008): 39.

80. Karl Barth, *Church Dogmatics, vol. IV*, 301, emphasis mine.

81. *Ibid.,* 301.

82. Eitel, "The Resurrection of Jesus Christ," 39.

83. 2 Cor 4:10-12, 17.

84. Andrea Bieler and Luise Schottroff, *The Eucharist: Bodies, Bread, and Resurrection* (Minneapolis: Fortress Press, 2007), 140.

85. Ibid., 63.

86. Ibid., 64.

87. Ibid., 138.

88. Brian Robinette, *Grammars of Resurrection*, 22.

89. Ibid., 23.

90. Ibid.

91. This comparative work has been taken up briefly by Ashok Collins, and an expansion of that work into a book-length project would be a wonderful addition to the scholarship.

92. Ibid., 120.

93. Ibid., 124.

94. Ibid., 135.

95. Ibid., 148.

96. Ibid., 149.

97. Ibid., 12, 24.

98. Ibid., 4.

99. Ibid., 333.

100. Ibid., 41.

101. See Nancy's response to Derrida, "Consolation, Desolation," in *Dis-Enclosure*.

102. Ibid., 42.

103. Ibid., 54.

104. Ibid., 65.

105. Ibid.

106. See Christina M. Gschwandtner's *Degrees of Givenness: On Saturation in Jean-Luc Marion* for a detailed account of the various levels of givenness to be found in Marion's study of the saturated phenomenon as an object of faith. Likewise, Ashok Collins' article provides a helpful comparison between Marion's and Nancy's methods.

107. Craig Keen, *The Transgression of the Integrity of God* (Eugene, OR: Cascade Press, 2012), 15.

108. Ibid., 20, emphasis mine.

109. Nancy, *Dis-Enclosure*, 60.

110. Ibid., 59.

Chapter Three

Eucharist, Prayer, Faith

The Body of Christ-the-Church

After the incarnation, after resurrection, Scripture establishes the *ecclesia* as the body of Christ in the world. Jesus himself proclaims this in the Gospel of Matthew, after his resurrection, and Paul, in his letters, elaborates on what exactly it might mean that a disparate body of believers may be the singular body of Christ in the world.[1] In particular, Paul utilizes the very metaphor of the body (*somatos*) to describe how Gentiles and Jews, people of different classes and social roles, could be considered one in Christ. The body of Christ in *ecclesia* is now *multiple*, spread throughout the Roman Empire (and now the world), comprising different classes, races, and cultures. This requires us to explore what exactly the *ecclesia is*. Specifically, we must distinguish between the Church as an institution, and the church as active *doing*. The Church-in-action is open for deconstruction, particularly the activities of partaking of the Eucharist (*eucharista*, or thanksgiving), praying, and actions taken in faith.

Nancy reads *ecclesia*, in "The Judeo-Christian on Faith," as evolving historically from a patriarchy of father/son to that of *brothers;* and from a static space like a temple to a nomadic *community*. He wonders "what the *koinonia* of our globalizations or becoming-global and its being-in-common in every sense of the term could mean."[2] As with incarnation and resurrection, Nancy's deconstruction of Christian tropes attempts to rescue what is worth "saving" from *ecclesia*, reading it against the grain of its own development, and emptying it of appeals to transcendence or salvation from elsewhere. The rise of Christianity was a historical anomaly: Religions typically arose out of cultural hegemony and sameness, and out of geographical locales. Christianity's spread as a religion that transcended boundaries of culture, class, race, and geography opened up possibilities of comm-unity, but also brought with it the rise of globalization and a leveling of difference in a dominant, imperial Westernization. To save the world from the latter, Nancy deconstructs the former, finding within Church practice possibilities for the "assembly" to work otherwise.

While there are myriad elements to the function and purpose of *ecclesia* in Western Christianity, I focus here upon three aspects that most directly apply to the Church as the body of Christ in the world. The partaking of the Eucharist—the body and blood of Christ—is an essential component of Christian worship, and most obviously involves the imagery, and in the Catholic tradition, the Real Presence, of the body of Christ consumed and consuming the assembly. While Nancy spends little time explicitly on the Eucharist, the Church itself understands its own formation as dependent upon the Eucharistic practice. Therefore, I open with an exploration of Nancy's brief encounters with the Eucharist, and then explore how the early Church understood its function, meaning, and consequence. I then look at modern feminist theologians to see how theology, from within the "church proper," re-interprets and deconstructs Eucharistic practice. Finally, I turn (again) to Craig Keen, and to William Cavanaugh, who read the Eucharist as the work of the Church in/with/among/by marginalized others.

Prayer and acts of faith present existential and ethical components of the Church in the world, and are areas that Nancy focuses considerable attention upon. Nancy unpacks what we may call prayer (or worship) primarily in *Adoration*, and addresses the issue of faith in various essays in *Dis-Enclosure*. He reads both prayer and acts of faith as gestures of relation that carry with them an ethic of justice for other bodies in the world.[3] In particular, Nancy reads adoration as an ethical, relational act seeking justice, and if we accept the notion that the Church, or any community, only "is" as it "does," we will need to apply Nancy's articulation of ethical being-with to *ecclesia*, and trace back his notions of comm-unity to the same. Therefore, this section will follow a different format than the previous chapters. Rather than fully exploring Nancy's work, then tracing it backward and forward to the early Church and current theology, I take a more thematic approach. Eucharist, prayer, and faith provide our three frameworks, as I follow Nancy's deconstruction of these terms, trace them to early Church writings, and explore current theologians' attempts to account for who the Church is being-with, and being-for.

THE BODY AND BLOOD OF CHRIST: EUCHARIST

What does it mean for the deconstruction of Christianity that Christianity founds the *ecclesial* body—the Church—upon the Eucharistic body of

Christ, whose born, dead, and resurrected body is the site of emptiness, of the absence of God? How do we move from Incarnation to Church, maintaining the claims made by Nancy? He does not devote much attention to the Eucharist. But the act of taking the body and blood of Jesus into the individual and corporate body is the founding conduct of the Church, so we will spend some time on the few times he does address it, expanding those seeds of deconstruction outward.

Hoc est enim corpus meum: Nancy and Eucharist

Nancy uses the famous phrase, *Hoc est enim corpus meum*, as his opening salvo in *Corpus*. Jesus speaks these words—"This is my body"—at the last supper, and subsequent Christian liturgy uses them as the centerpiece of the consecration of the elements, the bread and wine that become the body and blood of Christ. The early Church—and just about all subsequent denominations—hold the sacraments of baptism and Eucharist to be the essential means by which one becomes part of the Body of Christ, *ecclesia*. Nancy notes that for many Christians, the ritual of Eucharist is real consecration: Christians claim that "God's *body* is *there*," now.[4] Even those who do not hold to transubstantiation (the transmuting of the bread and wine into the actual body and blood of Jesus Christ) believe that the Eucharist marks out a space whereby one can commune, *co-mingle*, with the body of God. Nancy thinks this is a throwback to paganism, but nevertheless he notices that there is anxiety attached to these claims, both when the phrase is used ritualistically and sacramentally, and even when it is used in a more profane sense. In fact, he reads Western history and culture as echoing with this *hoc est enim* throughout the centuries.[5] Christians in particular are anxious to reassure themselves and others that this body is *real*, that you can *eat* it and be *certain*—or so Nancy claims.[6]

But what *is* this body? Or rather, Nancy asks, "who?" "*Hoc est enim* displays the body proper, makes it present to the touch, serves it up as a meal"—but even this proper presentation carries with it something foreign, weird, unreachable.[7] "We never get past it, caught in a vast tangle of images stretching from Christ musing over his unleavened bread to Christ tearing open his throbbing, blood-soaked Sacred Heart."[8] A drive or thrust (which he picks up as essential to adoration), accompanied by *un*certainty and anxiety, aims, in the Eucharist, to touch and claim *this* body of God, and this swirling conflation of desire, anxiety, and uncertainty forms the basis of what he calls "Western (un)reason." After all, as he points out briefly in "*Verbum caro factum*," the Eucharistic claim, the word Christ pronounces upon the bread and wine, is an *intensification* of the claims of incarnation.[9] Not only did God absent Godself in becoming a body, but that body, evidently, can become itself non-human matter (bread, wine). This is "mixing"—mixing of worlds, mixing of what should not be able to touch, first instantiated in incarnation, and then intensified in the sacrament of the Eucharist (the great thanksgiving). This is a *de*stabilizing claim, one that, in faith, one must believe without doubt, and yet one that requires doubt as one requires oxygen (for not to doubt is to have certainty, not faith).

From these few moments in Nancy's work, we must expand a deconstruction of the Eucharist. Given the time and attention Nancy draws to the act of prayer (*Adoration*) and faith (*Dis-Enclosure*), it is surprising that he does not do more with the Eucharist, which seems ripe for a deeper deconstruction. In order to do so, then, we will need to look at what Christianity has said, insisted upon, and most of all *performed* so that we may uncover the destabilizing effects of the consumption of the Eucharistic body of Christ.

The Early Church Fathers and Eucharist

The mystery of the body of Christ is not something Nancy is exaggerating; the same haunting question—How can this be? What kind of thinking is required to live in or with this sort of enigma?—rises in Christian thought at the very beginning. And, more to Nancy's point, this sort of claim *does something* to the history of the Western world. It introduces a strangeness. At this point it should not be surprising that the early Church Fathers did not avoid such questions, but rather once again intensified what Christians were called to live into. Again, rather than hiding in Gnosticism, Docetism, or any other alternative, the early Church insisted upon the *materiality* of Christ in the Incarnation, Resurrection, Ascension, and the Eucharist. Tertullian writes, succinctly, "Christ came in the body, died in the body, was resurrected in the body and ascended in the body to heaven. Now from heaven he fed his body on earth—the church—with his body and blood through the Spirit."[10] Seeking no escape from materiality and harshly condemning those that did, the early Church instead insisted that if the Incarnation was "beyond nature," then the Eucharistic bread and wine are also 'beyond nature.' Non-living matter made into the living body and blood of Christ was no great stretch, evidently, once one has claimed Incarnation and Resurrection to be true. From Irenaeus to Ambrose to Pope Benedict, the Roman Catholic Church, at least, has held firmly to the mysterious materiality of the Eucharist. Pope Benedict went so far as to write, "Christian belief knows no absolute separation between spirit and matter, *between God and matter*."[11] No separation between God and matter: One sees how the deconstruction of Christianity is made possible by such utterances.

Furthermore, the Eucharist was "resurrection food," a source of life for the body of Christ the church. Gregory of Nyssa in his *Catechetical Oration 37* writes, "Christ's *glorious* body which showed itself stronger than death . . . has become a source of life for us."[12] With the exception of Origen (later condemned) and Athanasius, the early Church through Augustine insisted upon the transformation of bread and wine into the actual body and blood of Christ, through which the baptized person would truly become one with the body of Christ in the world, the Church. Cyril of Jerusalem writes: "This one teaching of the blessed Paul is enough to give you complete certainty about the Divine Mysteries, by your having been deemed worthy of which, you have become *united in body and blood with Christ*."[13]

The early Church does not shy away from controversy and wild statements. See St. Ignatius of Antioch as he approached his martyrdom:

> I am God's grain, and I am being ground by the teeth of wild beasts in order that I may be found [to be] pure bread for Christ. My love has been crucified, and there is in me no fire of material love, but rather a living water, speaking in me and saying within me, 'Come to the Father.' I take no pleasure in corruptible food or in the delights of this life. I want the bread of God, which is the flesh of Jesus Christ, who is the seed of David; and for drink I want his Blood which is incorruptible love.[14]

Not only do we find the phrase "bread of God," which carries with it First Testament implications (manna in the desert, God as the bread of life), but here Ignatius claims that he himself is bread, or rather, is the grain from which bread could be made, and he would like, thank you very much, to be ground up for holy wheat. The martyrdom element is strong here, of course, but what is also striking is the refusal to metaphorically sugarcoat it: it is the *flesh* of Christ that is desired, and is to be consumed; Ignatius wants to drink Jesus's blood. It is no wonder the early Church faced rumors of cannibalism.

Likewise, Irenaeus, in *Against Heresies*, pushes back again Gnosticism by declaring:

> When, therefore, the mixed cup and the baked bread receives the Word of God and *becomes the Eucharist, the body of Christ*, and from these the substance of our flesh is increased and supported, how can they say that the flesh is not capable of receiving the gift of God, *which is eternal life*-- flesh which is nourished *by the body and blood of the Lord*...receiving the Word of God, *becomes the Eucharist, which is the body and blood of Christ* . . .[15]

The materiality of the Eucharist sustains the congregation's own material bodies, but more importantly, provides them with eternal life. The act of consuming the flesh and blood of Christ confers upon them, incorporates into them, the true body of Christ, which is now incorruptible. The fears of corruption and putrefaction (see previous chapter) linger here in the hope of the Eucharist, but they present themselves in a new way. Rather than this fear and disgust turning the Church toward rejection of all matter and all flesh as inherently corrupt, the Church pivots, insisting that (1) this flesh, this matter, is good because God created it; and (2) this flesh, this matter, may participate in the materiality of another, by Eucharistic partaking and by ongoing membership in the Church. My materiality is no longer simply mine (although again, fears of loss of personal identity pervade the early Church); it is taken over and infused by the Body of Christ in the Eucharist, and then my materiality is joined, retaining its uniqueness, to the larger body of the Church. My flesh does not cease to be mine, but it is no longer *only* mine.

John Chrysostom writes:

> This Body, scourged and crucified, has not been fetched by death. . . . This is that Body which was blood-stained, which was pierced by a lance, and from which gushed forth those saving fountains, one of blood and the other of water, for all the world. . . . This is the Body which He gave us, both to hold in reserve and to eat, which was appropriate to intense love; *for those whom we kiss with abandon we often even bite with our teeth.*[16]

One could write an essay on love as consumption on this paragraph alone, but for our purposes it is enough to see that this consuming, biting, tearing, and swallowing of Christ's flesh is tied to "abandon" and to love, to a gifting that is also an absenting, and to a love that is consuming and yet not consumed. The Eucharist, for the early Church, was a Trinitarian moment of intensification of all that Christian witness claims as truth: The Word of God is visited upon mundane elements via the power of the Holy Spirit, transforming those elements into the holy, material body of Christ, which is then torn and consumed by his followers, incorporated into their flesh, conferring upon them a kind of eternal life, now, in the flesh, and allowing them to form, as individuals, a collective body, unified by the blood of Christ.

One may rightly wonder how any group of people could convince themselves that this bread and wine were actually the body and blood—human, albeit sanctified, flesh—without becoming nauseous. A more skeptical way of putting the question is to simply note that the bread and wine at any number of altars and communion tables around the world persists in tasting, smelling, feeling, and even sounding like . . . bread and wine. Cyril of Jerusalem had a response to that: "For though sense suggests the mere elements, let *faith* assure you otherwise. Do not judge matter from taste but from *faith* be assured that you have been granted the body and blood of Christ."[17] While this answer satisfies no modern materialist, we will take up this notion of faith later on, as Nancy manages to articulate a kind of faith "in nothing at all" that may not redeem Cyril's claim, but may prevent us from engaging in the kind of snide dismissal that comes too easily to those of us marinated in scientific discourses.

As time went on, the Roman Catholic Church continued and intensified its adoration of the Eucharist as the Real Presence of Christ, insisting upon a *credo* articulating the firm belief in the Presence of Christ in the consecrated elements, instituting the feast of *Corpus Christi* in the thirteenth century (for which Thomas Aquinas composed hymns), and constructing chapels such that laypersons could worship near the tabernacle containing the elements. Adoration of the Eucharist intensified further during and after the Protestant Reformation, when again the Roman Catholic Church clung to mystery and insisted that the consecrated elements be "adored" for forty hours, or even "perpetually" (although there is much debate about what that exactly entails). Feast days were set up, decrees were written, etc., all focused intently upon the *adoration* of the body of Christ in bread and wine.

Of course we run into problems, then, when we bring this to bear upon Nancy's work on the same subject. The "grace beyond nature" that endows the bread and wine with, essentially, supernatural Presence, violates one of Nancy's most consistent positions: the lack of "outside" or "beyond" from which this grace might flow. Nancy both mourns this lack as something that *can* create a globalization or monoization of the world, and also seems to think that belief in this kind of externality leads to seeing the world as one (mono). The claimed existence of another world leads to viewing *this* world as singular, massive, the same. When we shift to understanding the world as instead suspended over a gap, a Nothing, a strange freedom opens up, freedom to be otherwise than just one. Multiplicity is given a chance to expand in a world with no outside. Of course, the more mystical aspects of the Eucharist must be ex-posed in a deconstruction of Christianity, but once again, when we perform this, we are not left with simply *nothing*. As such ontotheological elements are dismissed, weird stuff remains—most significantly, this insistent clinging to matter, materiality, bodies, that pervades Christendom in spite of itself.

Two more elements related to the Eucharist must be mentioned here, and pertain to the following sections on prayer and faith. First, the point of the Eucharist, which I have hinted at previously, is *unity*—not a massive, singular uniformity, but a comm-unity that is the multivarious body of the Church. The Eucharist provides the means by which each individual is offered eternal life, but also provides the moment where all share in the life of Christ as one body of many parts. Secondly, the partaking of the Eucharist is not meant to remain on the level of empty ritual, magical event, or pious practice. Augustine was most clear on this: The Eucharist calls each member of the body of Christ to a life of justice, mercy, patience, and faith. John Chrysostom was most clear, paraphrasing Matthew 25 and relating it to the partaking of Eucharist:

> Do you wish to honor the body of the Savior? Do not despise it when it is naked. Do not honor the church with silk vestments while outside you are leaving it numb with cold and naked. He who said, "this is my body," and

made it so by his word, is the same that said, "You saw me hungry and you gave me no food."[18]

As Nancy weaves adoration (emptied of theological import), faith (emptied of content), and an ethical call to justice for the bodies who share this space with us together in his deconstruction of Christianity, so too does the early Church, insisting that even the most "hocus-pocus" activity undertaken by the Church must be rooted in love and mercy for others—for their very bodies.

Modern Theology and Eucharist: Bodies in Christ

Feminist Theology

The Eucharist, both as eschatological symbol and as priestly act, has been taken up in the twentieth and twenty-first centuries by feminist theologians as a site of controversy and recovery. In *The Eucharist: Bodies, Bread, and Resurrection*, Andrea Bieler and Luise Schottroff explore the political and social ramifications of the Eucharist, writing "this book is about people who pray stammering but fiercely for the end of tyranny; it is about people who from time to time face death's dark shadows, and by doing so are confronted with their own helplessness and despair."[19] Secular readers may be surprised at the tone and focus—how does one read this much into bread and wine once a week (if that)? Once again, the answer is materiality—feminist theologians in general take up the materiality of Jesus Christ, and of the Eucharistic meal, and relate it to the suffering, broken bodies wounded and killed by state violence, by domestic violence, and by the more subtle violence of cultural norms. They address the effects of a market economy upon bodies, for instance, contrasting and interweaving the economy of scarcity and competition we live in, and the economy of grace and abundance suggested by the meal of the Eucharist. Food, originally the source of nutrition, is twisted by our culture into a far more ambiguous role: tied to maintaining a "perfect body," North Americans, particularly women, can find food torturous and shameful, for example. Politics and economics are not left outside the church door: Bieler and Schottroff seek to portray an alternative narrative to economy, food, and life itself via a renewed understanding of Eucharist. As they point out, Jesus himself was tortured and killed by the *state*, but his body was redeemed via resurrection—a economy the state cannot control, predict, or accommodate. By participating in the Eucharist, we participate in Christ's bodily reality (which is now in glory), and in the process our own bodily realities are redeemed. They write, "participating in this resurrection experience in fragmentary ways leads us *not beyond this world* in which bodies are subjugated to violence through systemic terror, malnutrition, and hunger.

Rather, the opposite is the case: body realities and food politics move to the center."[20] While certainly the assumption of God's presence pervades such a reading, the emphasis is not upon some "beyond" outside this world but rather upon the redemption *of* this world, now.

Bieler and Schottroff also interpret Jesus's words over the meal of the last supper through the lens of a body politic: "Object of political power grabs and ... of violence, marked with suffering and complicity—that is the body Jesus speaks of in his interpretive words over bread."[21] As Nancy reads the death of God in the creation of the world as well as the incarnation of Jesus, Bieler and Schottroff read the Eucharist as both the "renewal of creation *and* the resurrection of the dead*.*" Such parallels demonstrate the flexibility of Christian symbolism, allowing for multiple readings and interpretations, and expansions.

Similar to the early Church, Bieler and Schottroff understand participation in the Eucharist as the 'infusion' of our bodies into the body of Christ, and recognize the role of faith in such participation "as a relational act." Pushing against both the Gnostic and Cartesian tendencies to de-corporealize Christian practice and theology, they insist that there is no eschatology without corporeality, that the hope of the future is a bodily hope. Escapism is not Christian eschatology, or at least not sound Christian eschatology. Rather, as Christ was a body, so too is Christian hope in the body, each body.

Key takeaways from this reading of the Eucharist with regard to intersections with Nancy are threefold: (1) body materiality is insisted upon as the proper way to understand Christian doctrine and practice; (2) hope for the future (eschatology) is not escapist but rather is tied to the well-being of bodies, together with themselves and each other, in something like a relational ontology; and (3) Western imperialism, capitalism, and cultural norms are fundamentally violent to bodies, and must be resisted and counter-acted. While these theologians are obviously operating from under a different paradigm, and do affirm both the presence of God in the world and eternal life in resurrection, nevertheless their reading of Christian doctrine and practice recover and emphasize precisely what allows Christianity to deconstruct itself and the West, and open a future for bodies that is not monolithic, suffocating, and closed.

Bieler and Schottroff's approach to this topic is not the only feminist reading of the Eucharist. Susan A. Ross addresses the sacraments from a more critical feminist perspective, drawing attention to the ways in which women's bodies have been excluded from full participation in the sacraments (particularly in the Roman Catholic and Orthodox churches) in her *Extravagant Affections: A Feminist Sacramental Theology.*[22] Typically throughout Church history, women's bodies have been identified as material, as a site of a kind of dirty "body-ness." In current discourse, many churches' reliance upon gender essentialism as justification for the exclusion of women from ordination has raised real questions about the materiality of female bodies and how one might interpret difference otherwise. Feminists in general have criticized as well the assumption of duality—of body and mind as separate entities. But the adjustment that comes with the Enlightenment—in particular class liberalism—creates the fiction of the "universal human," which again avoids the body and bodily difference.

Specific to the Eucharist, the dependence and reification of the Eucharist as an 'atoning sacrifice' reinforces male-centric hunting/sacrificial rituals and practices, and concomitantly reinforces, rather than undermines, Western hierarchy and power dynamics.[23] Ross quotes Rosemary Radford Ruether on this point, who argues that "'[the] Eucharist should be the symbol of our nurture growth, and participation in the authentic human life of mutual empowerment.' But Eucharist, Ruether argues, has become a symbol for the preservation of clerical power [in the Roman Catholic Church.]"[24] In theory, but often not in practice, the Eucharist table is to be a place of equality, of the gathering of the fragmented body of believers into a fractured unity; but, particularly within churches that hold to gender essentialism and hierarchy (which is not limited to Roman Catholicism, but extends also to some Protestant denominations), Western imperialist gender norms are reified rather than deconstructed. Again, feminist theologians tend to read Church practices through sociological and political lenses, revealing that Church dogma carries with it real consequences for the flesh and blood of actual people. As such, such readings of the Eucharist reinforce Nancy's main claim that Christianity sowed the seeds of its own deconstruction.

Craig Keen and the Work of Eucharist

For Keen, separating out the Eucharist from the work of the Church is no easy task; indeed, Eucharist is in many ways *the* work of the Church, broadly interpreted. In various moments in his work, *After Crucifixion,* Keen refers to the Eucharist as "hospitality," "prayer," "a text," "a gift," and "a working." To participate in the Eucharist is to participate in a prayer that "one would be inscribed into the particular story of Jesus."[25] This work, then, becomes "a free *act of abandon,*" and the Eucharist is "that text in which their work is inscribed."[26]

The body of Christ, the Church, gathers together in its fragile particularity, its non-uniformity, its fragmentation, and together this body becomes the body of Christ through the reception of the gift, the hospitality, of Eucharist. The Eucharist does not resolve the fragmentation, remove the fragility, or make uniform what is diverse. Rather, more than anything, the Eucharist is, for Keen, an "active waiting," an act of waiting, a "getting up to let in the broken body and shed blood of Christ."[27] The Eucharist invites one in, but not to a solution or resolution or Hegelian concrescence with everything in its proper place. Rather, the Eucharist places our futures in "radical crisis," whereby we are the ones consumed by the body of Christ, not vice versa.[28]

In his earlier work, *The Transgression of the Integrity of God,* Keen also linked the Eucharist to the *work* of the Church, to the way the Church is called to work in the world. "In the liturgy of the Eucharist . . . we come to what we are created for: to gather the fruit of the earth and to offer it in adoration to its creator."[29] Obviously, the "outside" that necessitates this sort of theology would be anathema to Nancy's overall project; nevertheless, if we are looking to figure out what Nancy is doing with adoration, and Eucharist, and we recognize that he is not inventing out of whole cloth a way of being in the world, finding those tangential points of resonance is key to a more robust deconstruction.

William T. Cavanaugh: Torture, Politics, Eucharist

William Cavanaugh's remarkable and influential work, *Torture and Eucharist,* emphasizes the role of the Church as martyr in the world, imitating Christ's martyrdom against the powers of violence that dominate. He writes, "the church must offer its own self as sacrifice because the communion of Christ is nothing less than Christ's *corpus verum* . . . we become the body of Christ by consuming it . . . we then become food for the world, to be broken, given away, and consumed."[30] How he gets to this conclusion, however, requires some explanation. Cavanaugh's main focus is on the torture inflicted on Chile's own people by the Pinochet regime, and the role the Roman Catholic Church played in that situation as bystander. Cavanaugh's main question, that which drives his project, is "Jesus was tortured. Can his Body be redemptive for those who have suffered similar fates?"[31] How does the Church present an alternative vision and practice than that of the all-dominating, atomizing state? He traces the rise of the separation between church and state back to the crumbling of medieval, feudal society and the evolution of the state into the source of all power and definition-making, with the Roman Catholic Church in particular retreating from the political realm (by the twentieth century) and instead redefining itself as the "mystical" rather than "true" body of Christ in the world. By spiritualizing and individualizing worship, by making the Eucharist a spectacle to watch rather than a rite to perform, the Catholic Church in particular set itself up as, at best, utterly ineffective in the face of state terror and violence.

The role of the Eucharist takes center stage in Cavanaugh's exploration of religious imagination and a different (old, yet made new) vision for the Church in the world. He reads torture as the state's "perverted liturgy" or even an "anti-liturgy for the realization of the state's power on the bodies of others."[32] This anti-liturgy should be counteracted by the liturgy of the Eucharist, in which the body of Christ is *"enacted,* not institutionally guaranteed."[33] While "torture creates victims, the Eucharist creates *witnesses*," those who see, who mourn, and who work to save those who suffer.[34]

How could a rather arcane ritual, accused of being mere "hocus pocus," have such power of formation, such an ethic of care? Cavanaugh, as a Catholic, echoes the early Church Fathers over against later accretions regarding the Eucharist, and emphasizes that the role the partaking of the Eucharist played in the early (pre-thirteenth century) Church was one in which the believers gathered together *were consumed by* the body of Christ upon the altar, rather than consuming it. The Eucharist formed the disparate gaggle of Christ followers into the *ecclesia*, the *corpus verum* or true body of Christ in the world. "The Eucharist makes real the presence of Christ in both the elements and in the body of believers," who now form "the true body of Christ capable of resisting the discipline of the State."[35] The "Church" here is not the Vatican-centered Institution, with power and authority mirroring or at least attempting to mirror the power of the state. Rather, the church is merely these people, here and now, partaking of elements they, in faith, take to be the body and blood of a torture victim, resurrected, who undoes the order of the world. This undoing does not take place elsewhere, in some other world or realm divorced from this reality. Rather, the hope of the resurrected Christ, present in both the elements and in the *ecclesia*, is a hope for the peace, justice, and reconciliation of *this* world.[36] The *ecclesia receives* this Eucharistic gift, Cavanaugh argues (utilizing Jean-Luc Marion), and is "assimilated to the body of Christ," which is a "literal re-membering of Christ's body, a knitting together . . ."[37] In Cavanaugh's view, only this sort of performance of the Eucharist, this manner of seeing and touching it, can rescue the Church from succumbing to the power of the state either in capitulation or in retreat. Only this sort of understanding of the Eucharist makes possible "a body able to provide a counter-discipline to state terror."[38] As such, the Eucharist is an ethical act—partaking of it properly, accepting the gift, receiving one's changed identity into the body of Christ himself, enables the Church to both deeply feel the sufferings of others, and more importantly, stand with those others against the terrifying power of the state.

Obviously, Cavanaugh's high view of the Eucharist as Real Presence, his deep commitment to Catholicism, and his reliance upon a metaphysic of both time and space that require in-breaking and otherness make him an unlikely partner with Nancy. Nevertheless, the clarion call to stand with tortured bodies echoes Nancy's own deep concern for the piling up of broken, tortured, mutilated bodies, ground up and down by the powers of the West. Furthermore, rather than relying upon a metaphysic of stasis, Cavanaugh emphasizes the *act* of the Eucharist, the Eucharist as action rather than as "object."[39] Cavanaugh's reliance upon temporality as the main framework for his worldview, rather than spacing, also pushes against Nancy's nascent relational ontology. Nevertheless, one finds in his work a call for the *ecclesia* to be otherwise than the hegemonic power of the state, to provide not merely an alternative viewpoint, but an alternative community that resists monoization and instead embraces the fragmented, broken body of Christ.

The Eucharist is not simply or merely this strange incorporation of Christ's flesh into our own, but, via its consumption it instantiates the Church itself as a material body, a multiple singularity, *and* calls that body toward acts of justice and mercy. Becoming the body of Christ requires materiality and corporeality, not simply an infusion of the breath of the Holy Spirit (as at Pentecost). A physical body, multiple and singular, creating space in the world, *ecclesia* requires consumption, touching, incorporating—and that consumption is to take over this multivarious hydra and transform it into acts of love and mercy. In the next sections, we explore prayer and faith, other acts of the *ecclesia* that echo a kind of "being-with" we can perhaps rescue from the suffocating bonds of religion.

PRAYER

An Address to No One: Nancy and *Adoration*

Nancy seeks to save prayer and worship from religion—to save an opening that exists between us, that allows us to "*salut*(e)," rather than sending that "*salut*(e)" outward toward a heaven that is not there. He seeks a "salutation without salvation, which salutes existence" itself.[40] In his first volume on the deconstruction of Christianity, *Dis-Enclosure,* he claims that adoration is "prayer in its essence."[41] What do we salute, then? To whom do we raise the hand, the voice? To what do we address prayer? How does Christianity possibly introduce this possibility into the world in spite of itself? Nancy traces this out first via the Trinity: By positing God-as-relation, Christianity sets up God as an "atheist."[42] The relation is given from nothing and for nothing; there is only relation, no relator performing the action. As such, this relating-in-itself, in a decidedly non-Hegelian sense, is "gracious, generous, abandoned."[43] This "God"—this idea of God—is "*with*, not beyond or above . . . God is nothing other than this 'with'" which means "we with ourselves."[44] While this is a simple review for anyone familiar with Nancy's work, it is worth repeating that Nancy is not pulling this from thin air: Christian doctrine concerning the nature of God, the Incarnation, and the Trinity all call us toward a God of relation, "God with us" (Emmanuel), God *in* relation. Thus, it becomes clearer that one might loosen the empty noun "God" from all of this baggage and find oneself with a relational ontology, an ontology that makes no claims about beings except that we *relate.* And there is a kind of relating, a *responding*, that Nancy wishes to both trace and reserve beyond the death of the Christian religion.

Nancy first addresses prayer in *Dis-Enclosure*, primarily in a beautiful reflection on the demythologizing of prayer called for by Theodor Adorno. Recovering prayer from its religious overtones, from its ontological claims of a Presence or Being, is no easy task, and yet this is precisely what the deconstruction of Christianity is about. When one removes the object toward which prayer is oriented, what is left? When God is dead, to whom does one, and why would one, pray? Nancy centers prayer as fundamentally a linguistic act, as we are beings, after all, who *say*. Emptying prayer of an onto-theological object does not empty prayer of everything. Rather, prayer, Nancy claims, is at its essence a turning toward what I am not (an "outside," but not outside the world), a turning toward the real that is not me, and letting that be, even "adoring this letting be."[45] Adoration and prayer, deconstructed, do not speak to God and ask for something. Rather, they address the real before us. Ultimately, the goal of a deconstruction of prayer (or a prayerful deconstruction), saving it from the ties of religion, is to "open speech once again to its most proper possibility of address, which also makes up all its sense and all its truth."[46]

In *Adoration*, Nancy continues this attempt to rescue prayer/adoration/worship from the stultifying discourse of religion, while keeping it from being abandoned altogether by atheists. This ties into his non-ontology, or rather to his deconstruction of ontology, in which he moves us from stasis and Beings toward movements, actions, and relations. In every case, Nancy wants to preserve the Open, pushing against all trends to solidify, substantiate, locate, and close off the world via ideologies, ontologies, theologies, etc. Even as he sees, quite clearly, the role Christianity had to play in the creation of a monolithic/monotheistic world, and even as he is once again very clear that he is not here to resurrect Christianity, nevertheless, his tone modulates between mourning for what Christianity created, and a joyous seizing of the space provided by it. God's withdrawal, he says, "forms the ground of monotheism," which is bad, except that there is no longer any ground, which is good.[47] He strongly claims that he seeks "an exit from religion and of the expansion of the atheist world."[48] He sees Christianity's auto-deconstruction as creating that exit in spite of its static existence as a world religion.

The push of *Adoration* builds on his prior work on responsibility in *A Finite Thinking*. In both books, Nancy lays out a relational ontology grounded in no Being, but existing entirely in the between, the being-with, of existents acting and conducting themselves. Human beings have a special role in this web, in that we are creatures of language and thus are called to witness the world's existents, here to give account for the beings in the world.[49] We do not *discover* reasons for being, but *create* reasons for existence/existents via language. Language is who we are: "The gods who make us speak . . . are language through and through: they are names, myths, calls."[50]

What Nancy works hard to capture or at least give voice to is a non-theological account of responsibility and praise in community with others: not a civic religion, with no creed or belief, no structure or edifice. He seeks to make a robust argument that *this is the way the world is, now*. It is us. We are indeed thrown in the Heideggerian sense, into a world of uncertainty and trembling—but that is because *that is all there is: uncertainty, trembling, movement*.[51] We create the world by speaking: Our speech "relates existences to the nothing that is the ground" of the world.[52]

Yet adoration is not *nothing*. It is speech. It is a certain kind of speaking, too. It is not a defining, or a believing, or complacency, completion (which he calls evil). It is a response "to a call"—but this call does not emerge from the face of some Other, from a saturated phenomenon, from God Beyond Being. Like Levinas, Nancy retains responsibility, but his responsibility is consumed with obliterating any trace of an outside force, presence, or Being that would ground or pre-determine the world. Thus, human beings are infinitely responsible for the world, and infinitely called to respond to the thereness of the world-in-motion via adoration. The world is nothing more than "the open" we share, and we "must attempt to adore it . . . to address to it the witness of existence itself."[53]

Nancy understands human beings as relations—or rather, to capture the verb, as *relating*. We exist in that we are in relation with other existents, and this makes up the entirety of the world. Christianity opened the way to this, despite itself, by uniquely "representing its own essence as the incarnation of the divine"—by bringing that God Beyond Being into this world, as a trembling relation who lacks a ground, and in so doing opening up the possibility that there is no ground, has never been a ground, an Other, a World that guarantees our world.[54]

But one of the consequences of this lack of ground—and here is where Nancy sometimes sounds as if he longs for the good old days of paganism—is that there is no horizon for judgment any longer (we have lost the myth that there was, rather). Having no ground, no guarantor, means there is no sense held in common. Sense dissolves. And now we are truly thrown, and called to a responsibility for responding to this situation not with nihilism, nor with the worship of Reason in the place of God (like many New Atheists), but with, he says, "adoration."[55]

Adoration addresses nothing, has no object of worship, and, critically and against many other postmodern philosophers of religion, has nothing "facing" it. An ethic does emerge, however. If we are not simply to lie down and accept a nihilistic dissolution of sense, what are we to do? If we are not allowed to construct new idols, how are we to act? We are called, he thinks, to engage in intimacy with other existents, not *en masse* or as a mob, but one by one: "Here you are!" and, tellingly, "This is my body" are the verbal examples he provides. Adoration responds to the abysmal call of the bottomless, fathomless nothing that (un)grounds us all, and "desires this incandescence [of an Absolute nothing] for all beings."[56] Adoration seems to frame an ethic of desire, a responsible desire that celebrates the "unfurling" of the world, the rhythm of the world rather than the stasis of a statue, that salutes this groundlessness and also salutes the irresistible, irreducible relation that is each and every existent. Adoration cannot be *reduced* to an ethic, or a morality, but adoration is a kind of conduct, an activity that Nancy gently calls "spiritual."[57]

The Early Church and Prayer

If we read Nancy's parsing of adoration as tangentially akin to Christian worship, we enter into a fascinating kaleidoscope. Of course, all Christian worship is directed to precisely what Nancy finds both vacuous and dangerous—an existing God, the Ultimate Being, who exists beyond this world. But again—and this is beginning to sound like a broken record—Nancy's project is a *deconstruction of Christianity*. The material he works with is Christian, even as he unpacks, re-arranges, and dispossesses tropes, themes, and ideas from the source. So once again, we look to the early Church to see how they understand acts of worship and prayer, to find the points, of divergence to be sure, but also points of crossing, touching. In particular, we find some themes emerge: first, the lack of *completion* one finds in prayer and worship; second, the *responsive or compunctive* nature of prayer, and third, the *shaping of an ethic* that emerges from these acts in the Christian tradition.

Gregory of Nyssa writes, "Since no satiety in prayer is found, we are always burning with passion for God and stirring up the soul."[58] Many Church Fathers write upon the experience of prayer and worship, and emphasize the repetitive, indeed never-ending, nature of such acts. Christians are called to "pray unceasingly," to remain in contemplative motion toward God. Abba Isaac, in the fifth century, taught that monks should have "constant and uninterrupted perseverance in prayer . . ."[59] Likewise, John Chrysostom, in "Lowliness of Mind," urges his flock to remember that:

> For always and without intermission it is a duty to pray, both for him who is in affliction, and him who is in dangers, and him who is in prosperity—for him who is in relief and much prosperity, that these may remain unmoved and without vicissitude, and may never change; and for him who is in affliction and his many dangers, that he may see some favorable change brought about to him, and be transported into a calm of consolation.[60]

This unceasing motion of prayer cultivates a kind of character in the Christian, and develops virtues. That is, an *ethic* emerges out of this habitual behavior, a way of relating to self and to others. This praying is also a kind of *thinking*, for thought and prayer are not divorced from each other in the early church and Desert Father mindset. Prayer is a thinking toward God, or rather, a thinking called forth by the other, a thinking already in *response*. Abba Isaac taught, ". . . the mind in prayer is shaped by the state that is was previously in, and when we sink into prayer, the image of the same deeds, words, and thoughts plays itself out before our eyes."[61] We *sink into* this kind of thinking, and thoughts *play* before us, unbidden. The receptive nature of the act of praying, its direction and focus, its consequences, are each taken up and deconstructed by Nancy into secular forms. We are called to think, not by an Other, but by the very abyss and lack that lurks underneath all that is. We are *called* to think—this gaping lack calls forth response from us. And this kind of thinking elicits a kind of acting, a way of relating with the other existents lost, with us, in this world suspended.

Ignatius focuses on the kind of prayers called for from Christians:

> And pray without ceasing in behalf of other men. For there is in them hope of repentance that they may attain to God. See, then, that they be instructed by your works, if in no other way. Be meek in response to their wrath, humble in opposition to their boasting: to their blasphemies return your prayers; in contrast to their error, be steadfast in the faith; and for their cruelty, manifest your gentleness. While we take care not to imitate their conduct, let us be found their brethren in all true kindness; and let us seek to be followers of the Lord (who ever more unjustly treated, more destitute, more condemned?).[62]

The ethic driving this sort of thinking is clear: It is one that emerges out of the individual person engaging in adoration, and it carries with it a set of responses to other existents. One's prayers are not addressed to the self, or even to God, but ultimately one addresses one's prayers to and for others. In so doing, one's own actions are shaped and formed according to an ethic of love.

However, Abba Isaac is quick to point out that this kind of thinking is linked irrevocably to the existent (in Nancy's terms) *doing* the thinking/praying/adoring. Rather than an "institution" of prayer, or a course, or a model, the early Church and Desert Fathers emphasized the lonely uniqueness of each person, each body, called to wrestle with her own demons, her own vices, and called to think, rigorously and without ceasing, in her own way. Yet, in praying, each body is participating in the body of Christ that is the Church, for the *ecclesia* or assembly only exists *in action*, in a happening or moment of prayer, Eucharist, worship, faith, and love.

The early Church also centered prayer life around the Psalms of the First Testament. The Psalms, more than almost any other book of Scripture, were memorized and sung in worship regularly. Athanasius, a bishop in Alexandria and a key early leader in the Church, wrote a guide to the Psalms for one of his parishioners, which has both stood the test of time and serves as a guide even today. Athanasius himself was influenced by the desert monks of Egypt. As Benjamin Wayman writes, "Psalms is a kind of mirror of ourselves, which provides us with the words both to understand and express our deepest emotions."[63] These prayers, via the Psalms, "must be *lived*."[64] Simply speaking the words does no good—prayer, fundamentally, must be *enacted*. As words may witness and open space for us to be, as words may shape and give voice, prayer and adoration must be conducted, not simply thought. Athanasius claimed that praying the Psalms carries with it special purpose: "in the Psalter . . . you learn about yourself. You find depicted in it all the movements of your soul, all its changes, its ups and downs, its failures and recoveries."[65] Praying the Psalms ex-poses one to oneself, opens one up to the common failings and joys of others. "Just as in a mirror, the movements of our own souls are reflected in them and the words are indeed our very own." Praying the Psalms opens one to the in-common one has with others, and in speaking another's words, one finds one's own concerns echoed and even amplified. While certainly a willful act, praying, particularly praying the Psalms, may have unintended consequences.

This leads us to compunction. Prayer is not necessarily an intentional act of an existent. Rather, there is *compunction* in prayer, an arrival of praying to the devoted one. Christopher Hall describes it as "a reception of a kind of praying, a praying that seems to come from outside of the one praying. [It] cannot be manufactured at will."[66] Something *elicits* prayer, calls it out, draws forth response. While certainly for the early Church, that which elicits prayer is the triune God; nevertheless, this opening to a call from elsewhere, even if it is a call merely from the opening around me that allows me to exist, and others too, is not, even as emptiness, *nothing*. It, too, is gift.

For the early Church, prayer and worship were key activities of both the individual and the body. Prayer functions as more than just "self-talk," locked in interiority and circulating immanently. Prayer is an opening to the other, and opens one to that other. This opening that happens to the petitioner opens her not only to God, but to others in the world with her, calling upon her to act in faith, hope, and love. Perhaps adoration, deconstructed, maintains its ties to its concept of origin most strongly in Nancy. Pushing against the atheist tendencies to privilege interior Reason, and thus to create at worst individualized solipsism, Nancy holds fast to a kind of thinking that requires vulnerability, openness, and justice.

The Work of Prayer in Modern Theology

Craig Keen: Praying with Our Bodies

To analyze prayer in the work of Craig Keen ends up being potentially repetitive, in that he so tightly binds the Eucharist to prayer that we may end up simply covering the same ground. Nevertheless, it is important to emphasize that Keen even more tightly binds prayer to 'work'—and this word carries with it implications for Nancy's own understanding of prayer.

Rather than allowing prayer and worship to remain isolated interior thoughts, Keen places prayer in the world as action. But it is not just any sort of devout act, but rather *work*. "It is indeed to hunt and gather, to build and sculpt, to speak and think—all week long."[67] This weaving is to "unravel . . . outward to a world made new, an outside, an *eschaton* that liberates what was and is."[68] Again, Keen's reliance upon eschatology and the language of the "outside breaking in" seems to refuse to cooperate with Nancy's insistence upon "no other world," but I think this is not actually so. Salvation of the world is not annihilation of the world—the in-breaking is not destruction, and the *kenosis* of Christ places any such eschaton firmly in this lonely, only world we share. This eschaton is a *donation*, a giving in, a giving up in the world, not a triumphant return or a magical escape. While Keen's hope certainly, as a Christian, does reside in Christ (it has a home in Christ), Christ himself is *homeless*. To reduce eschatology to a kind of naïve hope or a magic trick fails to do the concept justice—at least it fails to do Keen's concept justice.

Elsewhere, Keen brings prayer back again and again to the body, to particular bodies, and in particular, to homeless and marginalized bodies: "The prayer in which she [an illegal immigrant] and they still touch does not float intangibly either above them or us."[69] For Keen, prayer is a witness to the life and horrible death of a Jewish peasant; to the life and often horrible death of the Mexican immigrant; to the life and often horrible death of the white businessman. Prayer is a witness and yet a hope, and a thanksgiving in the maw of that death, in the hope . . . of nothing at all. Church is hope *that gapes*. Opposed to the onto-theological structures and strictures of the Western mentality, for which Christianity stands responsible, is "another uncanny, irrevocably prayerful" way of thinking that does not seek to assimilate and fix the broken but rather to *defer* to them.[70] To be church, to *church*, is to "have a mind that opens to what is not and cannot be."[71] This thinking *opens*, it wounds the monolithic titan that looms over and as Western history, Western thought. As with Cheri DiNovo, it remains what it is not, defined by a kind of emptiness that is not a void. To be the Church is to engage in a precarious friendship with other broken people—and we are all broken people. It is to "again and again assemble, to enter into the Body of Christ who with abandon . . . gave himself to his neighbors."⁷² As such, to be the Church, is to be a "body practiced in the art of death and resurrection, love and sacrifice, of the work of the body and blood of Jesus Christ."⁷³

Thus, much in the same way that Nancy rescues adoration from empty recitation, bringing the work of language out of the interiority of the self and into the world with others, so too does Keen rescue prayer. While Christian prayer may address the God-with-us, if it *is* prayer and not mere spiritual narcissism, it must circulate in the space between my body and yours, and it must be lived out toward you in concrete action on my part. Prayer must break me open rather than shelter me, and open me to others. Only in this way is prayer in response to God in Christ.

Laurence Paul Hemming: Prayer as Being-With

This understanding of prayer as a breaking-open rather than an interior monologue is not only found in Protestant theology. Laurence Paul Hemming is a Roman Catholic theologian whose work focuses upon existentialism (and thus presents a different model of thinking than that of, say, Jean-Luc Marion). His use of Martin Heidegger and his emphasis on language as a site for ontology puts him in tangent with Nancy's emphasis on the linguistic element of human be-ing. In particular, his work on prayer enables us to hear, from an explicitly Christian perspective, similar concerns and similar structures to Nancy's deconstructive analysis of same.

Hemming, in "The Subject of Prayer," conducts a brief but masterful expose of the rise of the subject in Descartes and Leibniz. This territory is well-covered, of course, but Hemming adds to the discourse by demonstrating how ideas of God shifted due to the rise of the subject as the lever and measure of reason and indubitability. He asks whether there is an "ontology of prayer," and outlines an interior/exterior structure, derived from Descartes and Leibniz, whereby prayer itself has become interior thought, rather than lived practice. Descartes's move in the Third Meditation, whereby I know God because I first know myself, places God "in here," in me, rather than in the world. Leibniz completes this move in his monadology, in which he 'instrumentalizes' the body, completing its separation from the soul, and places God as the 'necessary substance' that underlies all individual subjective existence. God, rather than being outside the world, becomes a necessary component of my inner life, and thus prayer becomes a kind of interior thinking, separate from the world and entirely caught up within me. If I choose, of course, I may extend my prayer to others and with others, but the origin of prayer is subjectivity and interiority.

He sees this trend continuing, rather than dissolving, in the work of Martin Buber and Emmanuel Levinas. "Exactly as in Levinas and Buber, God occurs at the center of every intersubjective relationship."⁷⁴ God is the "transcendental horizon," or the "summation of will." "Subjectivity [becomes] the condition under which God might appear and become known at all."[75] God simply is the necessary ground or "between" from which human beings, in their interior lives, may have relations with other subjects exterior to them. The common ground is God (Buber in particular argues)—but this God serves merely as a construct, invented by Reason, and therefore is just Reason itself. He quotes David Lachterman (who wrote *Ethics of Geometry)*: God is just a "trajectory from mathematical construction to self-deification."[76] Prayer in this model is just a "method," not an event, a practice.

Once postmodernity, via Nietzsche in particular, removes God from the equation, we are left in self-isolation, a desolate subject with no ground upon which to meet, no star to steer by, no common substance. This echoes Nancy's own narrative of the fall of onto-theology: Nancy uses the word "sense' to indicate this common ground, and structures his argument differently, but Hemming and Nancy draw similar conclusions: We end up terrifyingly alone, with nothing at all held in common. Heidegger's not-fully-explored "being-with-one-another" is a direct criticism of philosophy's reliance upon interiority/exteriority and God as "between."[77] That Nancy latches onto this same point in Heidegger opens up a number of possibilities, which we will explore below.

Heidegger's move to destroy the construct of inner life/outer world via Dasein, "self and world belong[ing] together in the single being," sets up Hemming to rescue prayer from subjectivity and isolation.[78] To be human is to be "outside with" (notice the reliance upon spatial language). Relatedness is not a choice, or outreach, but the fundamental condition of our existence as existents. Hemming writes, "Together (really) we are open to the future that commonly and separately neither of us has."[79] Building upon "being-with," Hemming agrees, with Heidegger, that the interiority of the subject is a false construct, one that isolates, alienates, and destroys the world. With Heidegger, Hemming insists that we are in the world always, already. Rather than worship together being a choice one can engage in, there is only worship, together. "Prayer . . . is an event arising out of the ontological structure of a human person," and that structure "*is* being-with."[80]

How does this help us see postmodern theology in light of Nancy? First and foremost, Hemming begins his essay by placing prayer properly within language: "all prayer is my being inscribed into the Word of prayer, which through the Spirit returns to the Father."[81] Adoration is a kind of speaking, a witnessing of the world and of others to others and to the world—so Nancy writes, and so, from a Christian perspective, Hemming echoes. Human beings only *are* as they *act*, in *speech*, and prayer is an address to an outside that is not Outside, to an exterior that is not exterior, but is as intimate as breath. By breaking down the lingering effects of Cartesian subjectivity upon the acts of worship and prayer, Hemming opens the way for us to read prayer otherwise than as private speech, addressing a God I carry with me as a regulative idea or as a ground. God is not in me; if I think God is, I am only engaging in self-deification. But neither is God simply outside of me, for this structure is still dichotomous, and reinforces an ontology we are trying to escape. Rather, God is *with* me, not in the sense of Buber's between, which is just another subjective ground, but *as* the world, as us, with us, around us. This God is also, however, *absent*, in an onto-theological sense. While Hemming would hold to God-as-world, and Nancy would not (at least not with "presence" attached), nevertheless both thinkers argue for a non-onto-theological being-with as a site for human relation that does not rely upon a presupposed ground or foundation, but rather carries that foundation *as with*. And what is "with"? Where is "with"? It's nothing more than space, the space between you and me.

Keen and Hemming both wrestle with systemic questions as to prayer's efficacy; its intent and purpose; and with its possible locus within the subject. Whether approaching this question from a Catholic ontological-existential perspective, as Hemming does, or from a Protestant systematic theological perspective, as Keen does, both are deeply concerned with the retreat into subjectivity, with a loss of a sense of multiplicity-in-particularity, and with a deeper sense of belonging, of being-with, that the *ecclesia* was called to and lost (if it ever had it) as it rose to political dominance and ossified into institution. Prayer as an act of ethical relating, conducted by beings who are nothing but relating and language, and language-in-relating—this sort of prayer must be rescued from the stultification of Western imperialism, whether one holds oneself as a member of the *ecclesia* or not.

FAITH IN NOTHING AT ALL

Nancy: Faith as Gift

Although the order of the essays in *Dis-Enclosure* belies this, a good place to begin any exploration of Nancy's unpacking of the concept of faith is his more general essay, "The Deconstruction of Christianity," one of the earliest instances of Nancy addressing Christianity in this manner (first delivered as a lecture in 1995). Beginning here allows us to follow the development and focus Nancy brings to the topic over the course of over five years. Right from the start, Nancy defines faith as an act, not a statement, assent, or belief. A faith act may well be something like "pure intentionality" in a phenomenological sense, he suggests (although he makes it quite clear that the "saturated phenomenon" Jean-Luc Marion articulates is an object of worship, and is not what Nancy is claiming for himself or for this project). Faith has no object *per se*, but rather, in trust, it "exposes itself ... to absence."[82] Faith, after all, is in things not seen, and it resides in a space where proof does not. To have faith, then, to entrust, is to know no guaranteed object, no absolute recipient. Christian faith "misses itself, escapes itself" in that it exceeds any knowing, any certainty or confirmation. It calls out, proclaims, or supplicates—but it does so without foundation. This lays the groundwork for his more focused exposition in "The Judeo-Christian on Faith."

Faith is the primary topic of exposition in Nancy's essay on the Epistle of James in *Dis-Enclosure*. This letter from (possibly) James the Just, the brother of Jesus, dates from the early years of the Church (although, like everything about the ancient world, the dating of biblical texts is fraught with competing theories and controversies). Important to note for those unfamiliar with Christian scriptures is that this letter strongly emphasizes faith showing itself in *action*. James is unimpressed with those who claim belief and yet seem to be living lives in contradiction to those beliefs. Nancy's focus on this text, rather than any of the letters of Paul, is striking. Also striking is his deliberate and explicit use of a Derridean language of gift and giving to explicate the letter regarding this relationship between faith and works: good deeds, ethics. One needs to pay careful attention then, as it is easy to slip into a Derridean reading of this essay, rather than recognizing Derrida as one of the *subjects*.

Nancy begins to trace faith via the language of gift, writing, "To be in the image of God is therefore to be asking for grace, to give oneself in turn to the gift . . ."[83] This is, he says, the "Logic of faith."[84] For the first James, of the epistle, works *are* faith, and all faith is or can be is a kind of acting, be-ing (this correlates nicely with Nancy's understanding of relation in *Adoration)*. Nancy also indulges in the language of excess, a relative rarity for him (although not unheard of), arguing that at the "heart of faith [lies] a decision of faith precedes . . . and *exceeds* itself."[85] Just as James the Apostle argues, Nancy also argues that any sort of action that might be called faithful has nothing whatsoever to do with belief, with a rational mental assent to an idea. Simply believing in Christ is never enough, and in fact is not much at all ("Not everyone who says to me, 'Lord, Lord,' will enter the kingdom of heaven"[86]). Faith only ex-sists, stands up, or shows up in living action, an act that is an "ex-pos-ition . . . the sharing of the event as the opportunity of a becoming-self."[87]

Faith is far easier to recover or read against the grain of Christianity than perhaps prayer is. Or it simply may be that faith as a becoming of self, exceeds the boundaries of the religion called Christianity—that faith enacted, which is the only faith there is, is always nothing more than "an exhibition of inadequation/incommensurability."[88] Because faith is act in James, faith is both inadequate—always in response to the absent gift of God—and the "how" of existence. Faith is the act in which existents act their be-ing. This, Nancy claims, "decomposes religion even as it composes it: the untying of religion."[89] In James, we find a deconstructive articulation of faith, right in the heart of Scripture.

Nancy then moves to a different figure, one likely unfamiliar to many: that of Gerard Granel. Granel was a French philosopher who had great influence upon Nancy, Derrida, and others.[90] But again, the topic is faith, this time via an exposition of Granel's gesture toward a post-Heideggerian, post-Christian ontology. The James essay emphasizes that faith, whatever it is, is not static, not belief, and has no content. It is action taken in response to a gift received—and the gift, being the gift of Christ, is empty. Christ is the absent God *par excellence*. In the Granel essay, Nancy returns to his overarching concern: ontology.[91] Granel's path toward his coming ontology is fascinating on its own, for he was a Marxist Catholic who ended up both leaving the institution of Catholicism and yet was haunted by what lingers, or what may be recoverable from it. First and foremost, for Granel (in Nancy's reading), Faith is "a relation to a God who hides."[92] Faith is response to an absent God, not a response to a Present Being. Faith does not participate in onto-theology. Along with Nancy, Granel argues for an understanding of Being that is not "substantive" but "verbal"—Be-ing is language, is speaking. It is not a thing.

But how is this so? How could the very being of our being be words? Granel pushes past phenomenology's descriptive analysis and insists that the only "language game" that can capture or articulate "what is" is a kind of poetics, because Being cannot be grasped; indeed, in an apophatic way, Being is that which is ungraspable, because it Is Not. Thus, typical language games of logic and reason fail, because to articulate this absence in this way violates grammar and logic. But poetics, a kind of linguistic art, is able to perceive "Beyond Being as substance," and is able to say *something*.[93]

Nancy writes, "How do we recognize the ungraspability of being.... How do we touch the opening of the world? If not by a gesture ... attuned to the 'manifestly' divine aspect ... [a gesture of] neither knowledge nor certainty, neither objective nor subjective.... Must we not call it faith?"[94] If Granel's, and Nancy's, understanding of the world has weight, if we are to jettison God-as-Being, Being itself, Ground, Foundation, and One-ness, it remains an open question as to how human beings are to *live*. How are we to think without these ideals? How are we to resist nihilism? How are we to breathe, love, and from where do we get our concepts of ethics, justice? It is this kind of thinking that is both prayer and an act of faith for Nancy. Prayer and faith, recovered and read otherwise than in the Christian tradition, but nevertheless *found* there, may still guide us in this world. But in order not to simply reify what we have already cast away, they must be emptied of onto-theology, of static ontology, and of traditional Christian belief. That Christianity provides these means, these ways of relating, as well as the paths toward their deconstruction, may seem nothing short of miraculous.

The Early Church: The Incomprehensibility of Faith

But is this faith that Nancy reads into James and Granel the faith of the Christian tradition? Is this anything more than a sort of happy nihilism, celebrating the gap rather than mourning the abyss? How does Nancy truly get to claim that this is a deconstruction of Christianity rather than a reworking of twentieth century psychology with a dash (or more than a dash) of Nietzsche? The way toward the intersection of Nancy's deconstruction and Christian doctrine must pass through ethics. The early Church's own understanding of faith as *in action*, as that which shapes one's relating to others and to oneself, provides us the tangential line we need so that Nancy's own work does not appear to be vague or disconnected from the content of Christianity.

Ignatius writes:

> For I have observed that you are perfected in an immoveable faith, as if you were nailed to the cross of our Lord Jesus Christ, both in the flesh and in the spirit, and are established in love through the blood of Christ. . . . They (the Docetists) have no regard for love; no care for the widow, or the orphan, or the oppressed; of the bond, or of the free; of the hungry, or of the thirsty.[95]

Faith in the real physicality of Christ is what leads to ethical action of the real bodies of those who suffer. One cannot arrive at anything like faith without traversing the body of Jesus Christ, and this crossing does not create belief, or a groundwork, but rather elicits a giving. When one attempts to eliminate the body of Christ from Christian doctrine, as the Docetists do, one ends up unable to care for the world.

Likewise, the Desert Fathers tie faith to acts and deeds—to an ethic of being in the world. Otherwise, as in the Letter of James, our faith is nothing at all: "Our mouths smell bad through fasting, we know the Scriptures by heart, we recite all the Psalms of David, but we have not that which God seeks: charity and humility."[96] These are not simply theological virtues, but acts in the world, for others: "It is impossible that he who is of God should not love, and it is impossible for him that love not to work, and it is impossible to believe that he who teaches but works not is a true believer . . ."[97]

The early Church also distinguishes, as Nancy and many others do, between belief and faith, or certainty and faith. John of Damascus, in his *Exposition of the Orthodox Faith*, parses carefully between what we can know, and what we must 'speak' without knowing—indeed, what is unknowable may also be unutterable, yet we are called to speak faith. Operating out of an ancient cosmology (a closed system, rather than the infinite opening to/of space scientific discovery has exposed us to), John nevertheless insists upon a theology of the "absolutely incomprehensible and unknowable" God.[98] Indeed, he reads much like a negative theologian in the apophatic tradition, pointing out that what we say we "know" about God are simply things He is *not* (not begotten, not finite, etc.): "God then is infinite and incomprehensible and all that is comprehensible about Him is His infinity and incomprehensibility." While John devotes a lot of time to figuring out the exact relations of the Trinity, the way God may be simple and yet compound, and many other systematic theological elements that smack of onto-theology, he repeatedly returns to an apophatic position, limiting what is knowable about "God" and recognizing that faith resides in the infinite gap between knowing and "God." For instance, "The Deity being incomprehensible is also assuredly nameless. . . . For it is impossible for nature to understand fully the supernatural. Moreover, if knowledge is of things that are, how can there be knowledge of the super-essential?" A nameless, unknowable God who exceeds all words and all thought is the flip side of an absent God, nameless because non-existent, and unknowable because this God is not a thing, but a *gap*. Again, when John writes, "God, then, being immaterial and uncircumscribed, has not place. For He is His own place, filling all things and being above all things, and Himself maintaining all things," it is but a small step to instead read Christianity backwards on itself and see that this "no place" is an opening, not a filling; the Open, as such. And this space, this openness, ontologically speaking, is only "filled" by faith, and faith is an acting out and into this space with deeds of love and justice. Ultimately, even the most abstract systematic theology leads back to the requirement that Christians enact their faith in and as the world.

Finally, John of Damascus addresses faith directly, pulling from Romans and Hebrews to make his claims: (1) faith "comes by hearing"; and (2) "faith is the substance of things hoped for, the evidence of things not seen," which he calls the gift of the Spirit, not something a person may possess or claim as his own. Again, echoes of Nancy's deconstructive reading of James occur, as faith enacted is faith shared out, given away, rather than possessed.

Modern Theology: Faith-in-Act

Cheri DiNovo: Queering Faith

We return to Cheri DiNovo's book, *Qu(e)erying Evangelism,* to explore what the deconstruction of faith and hope look like from a postmodern Christian "queer" perspective. Again, DiNovo's main premise in this "how-to" work is to demonstrate the queerness of Christ in a meta-gendered manner, as going beyond gender but including it as well. In her last chapter, "Qu(e)erying the Gift," she references Derrida-via-Caputo in order to hammer home her point: that gift comes from the outside, not from us, from our political structures and present powers. "That we claim a gift given . . . is also faith, a faith similar to the new faith like the presence of deconstruction itself. The difference is that Christians call this hope beyond hope "Christ . . . but] it is critical that Jesus Christ finally and always, in this life, be undecidable, unreachable."[99] In an almost Levinasian sense, Christians are called to lives of justice, and that call issues from outside the will, or reason, or our own power. We are always already in response to a call that precedes us, that has always already been issued. In Nancy's terms, that other may be the person next to me. Nevertheless, a call is issued, solipsism is denied, multiplicity is confirmed, and monolithic oneness is rejected. How do we answer this call? "Only do what is impossible. This is how the queer Christian bows down. This is the queerness in the movement of our faith. This is how queer theology might work or unwork itself. What does it look like to pray to Christ, through Christ to God? . . . Prayer is an answer to the call from the other and the Other. It is an answer back. Again, it is not ours."[100]

This prayer, in the work of the Church DiNovo pastored, looks remarkably like a "being-with" of a comm-unity of disparates, of the marginalized with the powerful, the economically broken with the rich, the queer with the 'traditional." The body of Christ as the Church is, in short, a mess. It knows not where it is going; it cannot be sure of its actions; it is, in Nancy's word, "inoperative"—unable to achieve, promote, establish, fix, or transcend. It may, in fact, do not much at all. Nevertheless, it is not nothing—it is action, doing, adoration of what is not; it is hospitality. It tries things out, provisionally, improvisationally; it screws up, tries again, listens to voices from within and without. It welcomes the stranger, awkwardly but with good will, for the call has already been issued, and it is the Church's only job to, somehow, *respond*.

DiNovo quotes Michel Foucault as she tries to flesh out what it means to call Christians "queer." Foucault famously wrote, "It is no longer possible to think in our day other than in the void left by man's disappearance. For this void does not create a deficiency, it does not constitute a lacuna that must be filled. It is nothing more, and nothing less, than the unfolding of a space in which it is once more possible to think."[101] Nancy's relational ontology echoes this spacing, whereby the monolithic universal "man" is emptied out, emptied of God, emptied of one-ness, and this emptying, which Nancy reads as the auto-deconstruction of Christianity itself, gives us space to think otherwise. She uses this description to direct us to the rather poststructuralist phrasings of Paul, who insists that he is no longer himself, no longer a self, but is now a spacing in which something new is coming into play. Christians, in her estimation, are what they are *not*. "This is not metaphysics," she writes. Rather, this is about love: "The wounds of X are ours, and we, bleeding, can *then and only then* see the wounds of the other. The enemy of queerness is morality. Where flower words and romantic sentiments mask the terror of death, queers assert with Bonhoeffer, 'Death is the supreme festival on the road to freedom.'"[102] The queer church, then, "does not exist from the other or the Other. It exists to give itself away to the other, for the other."[103]

Rather than the monolithic, universal Church emphasized by a Christianity riddled with onto-theology, the marginal practices of churches, plural, reflect far more of a deconstructive approach. While retaining yet again the distinction of faith in that which is outside the scope of the world, postmodern Christian practice seeks to undo belief in structuralism, in God-as-Being, and in wholeness and uniformity. As such, and as one would imagine, such churches are local, particular, and usually looked upon with suspicion by any governing denomination. At times, such churches lose that affiliation altogether, as they are unwilling to embrace the structural, separatist and yet uniformist rhetoric of established religious institutions. Yet they still live on under the sign of Christ (X), even while acknowledging that sign as an absence. What is it to be Church—the body of Christ? Is there a way Christian faith may walk with deconstruction, agreeing to disagree about some terminology but embracing, co-embracing, the fragility of being-with?

Craig Keen: Faith in Fear and Trembling

Once again, we find ourselves entangled in terms that relate, correspond, and traverse each other, such that teasing them out is exhausting. Nevertheless, Keen and Nancy share such similar terms and perspectives, it becomes near-impossible to have a chapter without Keen in it, however briefly. Keen, in various essays, writes on faith. To live in and as this Church, to be a particular body in this particular body, is to "have faith," but not as a possession. Faith is elusive, *an act,* not a thing. He quotes Alexander Schmemman, an Eastern Orthodox theologian, who writes that faith is "contact and a thirst for contact, embodiment and a thirst for embodiment; it is the operation of one reality within another."[104] Faith is faith in the gap, the gaping, the space that opens in the death of the Jewish peasant, in the believed-upon resurrection of that peasant, wounds still gaping. It is not a doctrine, nor anything to cling to. It does not provide a foundation upon which to stand, or a ground onto which to leap. Rather, faith is a stepping out.

Focusing upon the work of John Wesley, Keen asks a number of key questions that open up faith as more-and-less than assent, belief, or choice:

> What if faith had nothing to do with "experience," with the appearing of a phenomenon in the consciousness of an apprehending subject? What if faith were not found anywhere in particular *in me*? What if faith were seeing in the mode of being seen, knowing in the mode of being known? What if faith were the gift of life, of an opening out into a future not to be achieved, but coming...?[105]

Similar to Hemming's existential analysis of prayer, Keen refuses the subject/object dichotomy of Descartes, rejects the notion of an apprehending subject who owns, possesses, and holds opinions and beliefs. Receptive rather than active, receiving rather than dominating, the call of faith for a Christian is a call out of oneself into a state of "active waiting upon God."[106] Rather than the possession of belief, faith is a giving away. Rather than a guarantee, faith is a radical risk. Rather than a knowing, faith may be being known, but in such a way that one cannot claim certainty about even that. Keen's understanding of faith, informed in no small way by the works of Søren Kierkegaard, seem to model the very sort of deconstruction Nancy claims needs doing.

Of the many subjects touched upon in Nancy's deconstruction of Christianity, faith seems at once his most positive project, and his most slippery. In spite of having essays that ostensibly focus entirely upon it, faith for Nancy ends up in a non-definitive space. One hesitates to use phenomenological language like "intention" to describe it (although there is great work to be done on that); one also wants to avoid over-psychologizing it as "disposition" or "orientation." Nevertheless, for Nancy, faith—even in nothing at all—pushes back against nihilism and cynicism, refuses to give up in the face of a brutalizing world, and insists that this world we share is *enough*. This world, these spacings, are *worth it*.

Eucharist, prayer, faith: these are three components or enactments that open up the community called *ecclesia*, or Church. This assembly or gathering was never formed by charter, nor even, as Nathan Kerr writes, "by the invocation of some ambiguous beyond, but precisely by the pneumatic call of this very *world* as it is being transformed by the occurrence of that which is, eschatologically speaking, an event *neither* or the church *nor* of the world in any strict sense of those terms."[107] The Church only exists in and as the world—there is no other. While an in-breaking of the spirit, in the eschaton, is *hoped* for, Christians are called not merely to hope, but to live out that in-breaking *as if* it has already occurred. Indeed, in faith, Christians claim that in one sense it has, via the incarnation, death, and resurrection of the body of Christ. The acts of partaking of the broken body of Christ, of witnessing the opening between us as a space of giving and breathing, and of a wild trust in the impossible: All these acts are the works, the working, of the *ecclesial* community, if it is worthy of the name. "There is no *ecclesia* apart from our being bound by the spirit to *this* world, for only as such are we truly *gathered* into the apocalyptic 'sending' that is Jesus himself."[108]

In some ways, separating Eucharist from prayer from faith is a vicious act of dissection. While from the outside they may seem like disparate actions, with very different structures, goals, and functions, in practice, partaking of Eucharist (thanksgiving) is an act of prayer, and an act of faith; working for peace and justice in the world is an act of prayer and of Eucharist. The Church surely has forgotten its calling innumerable times over the course of centuries. It has failed, and will fail again. To deconstruct these terms is an act of service to the church, frankly, in many ways: Ideally, it would remind those "in the faith" of the real work *ecclesia* must do if it may legitimately claim that title. Nancy's examination of adoration, faith, and Eucharist enable the Church to recover its past, and perhaps live in its present, but not as a dominant political force, as the "moral majority," or by controlling the halls of power. The Church's call is to be fragmented, as the body of Christ is fragmented; to be broken, as the body of Christ remains broken; to feed and to clothe and to heal, as the body of Christ did and commanded his followers to do.[109] The Church as the body of Christ is no monument darkening the horizon. It is my hand outstretched to the body next to mine.

Nancy's deconstruction of the Church is scattered across his many works; the works themselves interrupt themselves, carry other voices with them, and refuse order. Nevertheless, through these three essential actions of the *ecclesia*—acts that, indeed, *make* the *ecclesia*—he is able to uncover or recover faith and prayer (and with them we uncovered the Eucharist) from a Western imperial onto-theology state or stasis, casting such actions into a world emptied of God, but not emptied of meaning, or of hope, or of justice. Would that the Church, now, recover these ways of being-with as well.

NOTES

1. I have chosen to use the Greek word *ecclesia* regularly throughout this chapter in order to keep us from slipping into assumptions. The word "church" carries with it any number of stereotypes, and is also of course used nowadays to mean both a building, a congregation, and a denomination, as well as the "church universal." *Ecclesia* in the Greek means something like "assembly" or "gathering," a far looser term that carries with it a sense of event rather than institution. Simply put, *ecclesia* puts more into play than "church" may for the English speaking reader. See Matthew 28:18-20 NRSV: "And Jesus came and said to them, 'All authority in heaven and on earth has been given to me. Go therefore and make disciples of all nations, baptizing them in the name of the Father and of the Son and of the Holy Spirit, teaching them to observe all that I have commanded you. And behold, I am with you always, to the end of the age.'" See Ephesians 1:22-23; 2:19-22, 5:25; 1 Corinthians 12:12-14, and Colossians 1:17-20. NRSV.
2. Nancy, *Dis-Enclosure*, 45.
3. Nancy certainly calls for responsibility with others, but rejects the transcendence Levinasian philosophy sets as its main priority.
4. Nancy, *Corpus*, 3.
5. Nancy, *Corpus*, 5.
6. Certain of what, exactly, Nancy does not specify.
7. Ibid.
8. Ibid.
9. Nancy, *Dis-Enclosure*, 81.
10. Christopher A. Hall, *Worshiping with the Early Church Fathers* (Downers Grove, IL: IVP Academic, 2010), 53. Quoting Tertullian from "On the Resurrection of the Flesh," 8.
11. Hall, *Worshiping*, 56, emphasis mine.

12. Hall, *Worshiping*, 61. One may notice the word "glorious," mentioned in the previous chapter.
13. Cyril of Jerusalem, "Homily 22," *New Advent*, accessed November 1, 2016, http://www.newadvent.org/fathers/310122.htm.
14. Ignatius, "Letter to Romans 7:3," *New Advent*, accessed November 1, 2016, http://www.newadvent.org/fathers/0107.htm.
15. Irenaeus, "Against Heresies 5:2:2-3," *New Advent*, accessed November 1, 2016, http://www.newadvent.org/fathers/0103.htm.
16. John Chrysostom, "Homilies on Corinthians 8, 1[2]; 24, 2[3]; 24, 2[4]; 24, 4[7]" in William A. Jurgens, *The Faith of the Early Fathers, Volume 2*. (Minnesota: The Liturgical Press, 1979), 117-119.
17. Cyril of Jerusalem, "Catechetical Lectures, 22, 23," *New Advent*, accessed November 2, 2016, http://www.newadvent.org/fathers/310122.htm.
18. John Chrysostom, "Homilies on the Gospel of St. Matthew, 12," *New Advent*, accessed November 2, 2016, http://www.newadvent.org/fathers/200112.htm.
19. Andrea Bieler and Luise Schottroff, *The Eucharist: Bodies, Bread, and Resurrection* (Minneapolis, MN: Fortress Press, 2007), 2.
20. Bieler and Schottroff, *The Eucharist*, 3, emphasis mine.
21. Bieler and Schottroff, *The Eucharist*, 139.
22. Susan A. Ross, *Extravagant Affections: A Feminist Sacramental Theology*. (New York: Continuum Publishing Company, 1998).
23. Ross, *Extravagant Affections*, 120.
24. Ross, *Extravagant Affections*, 87.
25. Craig Keen, *After Crucifixion*. (Eugene, OR: Cascade Press, 2013), 17.
26. Keen, *After Crucifixion*, 17, 104, emphasis mine.
27. Keen, *After Crucifixion*, 47, 64.
28. Keen, *After Crucifixion*, 14-15.
29. Craig Keen, *The Transgression of the Integrity of God*. (Eugene, OR: Cascade Press, 2012), 81.
30. William T. Cavanaugh, *Torture and Eucharist*. (Malden, MA: Wiley-Blackwell Publishing, 1998), 231-32.
31. Cavanaugh, *Torture and Eucharist*, 1.
32. Cavanaugh, *Torture and Eucharist*, 12, 206.
33. Cavanaugh, *Torture and Eucharist*, 221.
34. Cavanaugh, *Torture and Eucharist*, 206.
35. Cavanaugh, *Torture and Eucharist*, 205-206.
36. Schmemann writes, ". . . not another world, difference from the one God has created . . . it is our same world already perfected in Christ, but not yet in us" (13).
37. Cavanaugh, *Torture and Eucharist*, 229.
38. Cavanaugh, *Torture and Eucharist*, 229.
39. Ibid., 213.
40. Nancy, *Adoration*, 64.
41. Nancy, *Dis-Enclosure*, 136.
42. *Adoration*, 31.
43. Ibid., 32.
44. Ibid., 41.
45. *Dis-Enclosure*, 136.
46. Ibid., 138.
47. *Adoration*, 44.
48. Ibid., 22.
49. Ibid., 67.
50. Ibid., 68.
51. Ibid., 67.
52. Ibid., 68.
53. Ibid., 70.
54. Ibid., 71.

55. Ibid., 74. Examples of the former are numerous. Richard Dawkins writes, "The feeling of awed wonder that science can give us is one of the highest experiences of which the human psyche is capable. It is a deep aesthetic passion to rank with the finest that music and poetry can deliver." Likewise, "I believe that an orderly universe, one indifferent to human preoccupations, in which everything has an explanation even if we still have a long way to go before we find it, is a more beautiful, more wonderful place than a universe tricked out with capricious, ad hoc magic." *Unweaving the Rainbow: Science, Delusion, and the Appetite for Wonder.* (New York: Mariner Books, 2000), x-xi.

56. Nancy, *Adoration,* 78.
57. Ibid., 86.
58. Gregory of Nyssa, "On the Christian Mode of Life," in Christopher Hall's *Worship of the Early Church Fathers,* 82.
59. Abba Isaac, in *The Conferences of John Cassian,* ed. Edgar C. S. Gibson, accessed November 2, 2016, http://www.osb.org/lectio/cassian/conf/book1/conf10.html#10.10.
60. John Chrysostom, "Lowliness of Mind," *New Advent,* accessed November 1, 2016, http://www.newadvent.org/fathers/1907.htm.
61. Abba Isaac, *The Conferences.*
62. Ignatius, "Letter to the Ephesians," *New Advent,* accessed November 2, 2016, http://www.newadvent.org/cathen/12345b.htm.
63. Wayman, *Make the Prayers Your Own,* xvii.
64. Ibid., xx.
65. Athanasius, "The Letter of Athanasius to Marcinellis," *New Advent,* accessed November 11, 2016, http://www.athanasius.com/psalms/aletterm.htm.
66. Hall, 106.
67. Keen, *Transgression,* 45.
68. Ibid.
69. *After Crucifixion,* 4.
70. Ibid., 11.
71. Ibid.
72. Ibid., 104.
73. Ibid., 188.
74. Hemming, "The Subject of Prayer," in *Blackwell Companion to Postmodern Theology,* ed. Graham Ward (Malden, MA: Blackwell Publishers, 2001), 448.
75. Ibid., 449.
76. Ibid.
77. Hemming goes so far as to say that the ethics of Buber and Levinas always end up with one subject sovereign over another—even in my submission to the Face of the Other, I win, "I triumph through dis-empowerment." Ibid.
78. Ibid., quoting Heidegger.
79. Ibid., 453.
80. Ibid., 455.
81. Ibid., 445.
82. *Dis-Enclosure,* 153.
83. Ibid., 50.
84. Ibid., 51.
85. Ibid., 52.
86. Matthew 7:21, NIV.
87. *Dis-Enclosure,* 53.
88. Ibid., 58.
89. Ibid., 60.
90. Nancy wrote a book on his works, not translated into English, titled *Granel - l'éclat, le combat, l'ouvert,* in 2001, and this essay is taken from that larger work.
91. One could say that Nancy's work as a whole is twofold: to save the world from both religion and ontology. Indeed, in many ways they work in fundamentally the same ways.
92. Ibid., 63.

93. But, Nancy points out, Granel has backed himself into a corner here. Granel insists he wants to "go farther," to surpass Heideggerian metaphysics and phenomenology. To do so, he must describe this experience of a world appearing to me without me "appropriating" it, *and* without being appropriated *by* it. How do I speak of the world without defining it, representing it, and thus flattening out all that is diverse, ephemeral, moving, transitory, and beautiful? Granel tries to circumvent this problem in a way Nancy would find much sympathy with: by appealing to a relational (or in this case linguistic) ontology of *space* rather than *time*.

94. Ibid., 73.

95. Ignatius, "Epistle to the Smyrnaeans," *Patristics,* accessed November 3, 2016, http://www.patristics.co/2016/02/21/ignatius-epistle-to-the-smyrnaeans/.

96. A passage found in most collections of the teachings of the Desert Fathers. Believed to be from the 4th century. See Benedicta Ward and Anthony Bloom, *Wisdom of the Desert Fathers.* (Collegeville, MN: Cistercian Publications, 2006), 29.

97. E. A. Wallis Budge, *The Paradise of the Holy Fathers.* (Seattle, WA: St. Nectarios Press, 1984), 262-263.

98. Translated by E. W. Watson and L. Pullan. From *Nicene and Post-Nicene Fathers, Second Series,* Vol. 9. Ed. Philip Schaff and Henry Wace (Buffalo, NY: Christian Literature Publishing Co., 1899.) Revised and edited for *New Advent* by Kevin Knight, accessed November 10, 2016, http://www.newadvent.org/fathers/33041.htm.

99. Cheri DiNovo, *Que(e)rying Evangelism: Growing a Community from the Outside In.* (Cleveland, OH: Pilgrim Press, 2005), 181.

100. Ibid., 183.

101. Ibid., quoting Michel Foucault, *The Order of Things*, 25.

102. DiNovo, 25.

103. Ibid., 28.

104. Keen. *Transgression,* 39.

105. Ibid., 99.

106. Ibid., ft37, 61.

107. Nathan Kerr. *Christ, History, and Apocalyptic: The Politics of Christian Mission.* (Eugene, OR: Cascade Press, 2009), 190.

108. Ibid.

109. Matthew 25.

Why Christianity?

One of the most powerful aspects of Jean-Luc Nancy's work in and around deconstruction throughout his life has been the moral urgency of his projects. Those from outside the discipline of philosophy often deride this work as impenetrable gibberish without a point, as a kind of performance without end or purpose. And I am sure we can admit privately that there are some works out there that just might be guilty of this charge. But at its best, deconstruction (and phenomenology) is driven by a call to justice, or mercy, a call from the margins that begs for someone to listen. Deconstruction, at its best, rescues new meaning from old accretions, finds novelty and freedom from within not just "outsider" work, from within even hoary, accepted, traditional philosophy. Nancy carries on with this ethical response to a call. He hears, from within the canon of Christian thought, a reading and a writing that slants, that undermines the possible monolith of Christendom and undoes, from within, the prison of the world.

But why Christianity? Like Plato, Christianity has served as a firm foundation for this history of Western thought. It *is* Western thought, and therefore if we are to escape its hegemony, it will only be by digging ourselves out. Novelty and rescue will not drop from above like a *deus ex machina*—the only way out of the catastrophe of the West is via its own texts. Nancy's project, therefore, is not merely mental gymnastics, nor merely a tear-down project. As serious as Nancy is that he wants a non-theistic, immanent world of being-with, without God, without Outside, without religion, when the text is as complex, and historically accreted, as Christianity, one cannot set up the text simply as a failure. This is why we find the back-and-forth tension in Nancy's work—just as he strongly states that he seeks no recovery or rescue of Christianity or indeed any religion, nevertheless we are dependent upon these Christian traces for the world he wishes to see. Whatever kind of adoration we will be able to perform, whatever witness we can be to the marginalized bodies of others, and to our own flesh, will be constructed, repurposed, from the wreckage we inherit. There is truly nothing new under the sun—except what human beings make from what we have. For better or worse, we have Christianity.

And despite our fears and disgust with this inheritance, Christianity more than any other monotheism, it seems, provides us with the richness, the traces, we need. I have attempted in this work to unpack this multiplicity, to trace Nancy's deconstruction of Christianity back to Christian doctrine itself, not only to demonstrate to some that his work is not wildly off the mark or some sort of postmodern hocus pocus, but to reveal in a positive sense how much more work there is to do. Christian thought takes common tropes such as divine incarnation, resurrection, and community-formation and explodes and multiplies them, layering claim after claim upon the single, fragile body of a Jewish peasant, which now, like Atlas, bears the world upon his shoulders. I have tried to show as well that Nancy's claim that Christianity auto-deconstructs itself is well-founded, that more than perhaps any other aspect of our modern inheritance, Christian thought provides us with pathways and traces worth pursuing.

The body of Christ "sinks beneath our wisdom like a stone."[1] The multiplying of the body of Christ in Christianity is truly extraordinary. I hope that I have been able to demonstrate just how complex this single trope is. The world in creation is the body of the absent God; the person of Jesus is the frail, bloody, beaten body of God-as-absent; the resurrected body of Christ is absencing-in-motion, is the standing-up of death itself. The supernatural body and blood of Christ lies upon the altar as bread and wine; the Church, as the body of Christ in this world, is brought into existence by the consumption of that body of Christ, which itself is brought into possibility by the resurrection and ascension of the body of Christ, which itself depends upon the incarnation of Christ. . . . We can move back and forth along this strand, this trace, encountering bodies upon bodies. And the body of Christ in *ecclesia* is also multiple, fragmented, broken, and sometimes bleeding. It is, after all, made up only of human bodies, themselves singular multiplicities, containing multitudes. Nancy's works on community and *mitsein*, "being-with," amplify these singular multiplicities as opposed to globalization and the universalizing tendencies of monotheistic religion. In *Corpus, The Inoperative Community*, and other works, Nancy draws us back to the fragmented diversity that is, loosely speaking, the world, and encourages us to think beyond the stultifying "common sense" of religion to a more human, more humane space (or "spacing") that allows bodies to *be*.[2] That we find such multiplicities in the doctrines of one of those "common sense" monotheisms is striking, and strangely hopeful.

This theme is merely one path through Christian thought, one possible deconstruction. I hope I have managed to weave together some of the sources of this deconstruction, so that readers of various persuasions—philosophical, theological, Christian, secular—may see that Nancy's work is operating upon this rich legacy, that this truly is a deconstruction of *Christianity* itself. From a theological perspective, this work aimed to demonstrate that deconstruction is a legitimate, indeed necessary, method for thinking the Christian faith. Deconstruction tries to *discover*, not *destroy*, the texts upon which it operates. Christianity as a political force in the world has much to atone for, and Christian doctrine has been used for domination, the silencing of marginalized voices, and to justify physical violence. Yet the heart of Christianity is not or should not be such actions. And we, from within the faith, know it. The deconstruction of Christianity need not be a threat (although plenty of people would like it to be). It is an opportunity, rather, for atonement, and for a rediscovery of what I have very professionally called the "weirdness" of the Christian faith. Christianity claims strange things; it insists upon paradox and contradiction. Deconstruction helps us to see this, again, to recover what is lost when we focus upon building inviolable edifices of doctrine and might rather than living out "queer" lives of love and mercy.

Christianity is indeed ripe for deconstruction. Our collective inheritance provides us with rich resources for understanding and for creative possibility. In spite of the hegemony of Church dominance for centuries in the West, in spite of inquisitions and genocides in the spirit of oneness, the inexhaustible remains of Christianity provide us with material fecund even in its dissolution. Of course, one can deconstruct almost anything, provided it be rich enough, textually thick enough, to make the project worth one's while. For sheer depth of field, sheer possibility of tracing, the beyond-reason scope of Christian belief and thought seems almost inexhaustible for deconstruction. Perhaps this is what modern a/theists find so frustrating—we never seem to finish, to finally be done with it. When can we move on?

I do not know that we can.

In *The Inoperative Community,* Nancy issues forth a scathing critique of Christianity, reading it as "the Empire depoliticized and rendered moral," as the last gasp of an odious god. Yet what follows this take-down is a paragraph-long parenthetical "and yet . . ." He writes:

> (In the end, something resists. To all of the harshest and most justified criticism of Christianity—of its political and moral despotism, its hatred of reason as much as of the body, its institutional frenzy or its pietistic subjectivism . . . to all of that something puts up a resistance . . . something that, it is not impossible to claim, has left upon the form of the *Pater noster* . . . a mark that is difficult totally to erase: a generous abandonment to divine generosity . . .)[3]

The criticism is not wrong. The history of Christianity is the history of the West, and it is, as Nancy has made very clear, a story of domination, globalization, the depersonalization of the human being, the commodification of the body and labor, the reduction of communal life to an empty solipsism, ecological disaster, and on and on. One cannot untangle Christianity from this history and redeem it. Yet one can untangle the political institution of Christendom (to borrow from Kierkegaard) from the small actions taken by people who find themselves in something like, in spite of everything, *community*, in the hopeful yet fragile sense Nancy describes it in this same work.

Nancy writes in *The Inoperative Community* that we "miss" community because the thinking of the West focuses upon essence, ideal, and atomistic individuality, and forgets relation, the "inclination or an inclining from one toward the other" of an individual.[4] While the "absolute" of Hegel, or the ideal of the state, all presume singularity, real community "cut[s] into this subject . . . is . . . nothing other than what it undoes."[5] In recognizing this, the unified Being of monotheism is undone: "Being 'itself' comes to be defined as relational . . . *as community.*"[6]

Christianity has played a crucial role, of course, in the setting up of unity, unicity, fraternity, etc., as the definition of community. In each instantiation, into the modern era, the goal of community has been a subsuming of particularity into unity. The fantasy of the "lost" community—a mythical time when human beings were truly fraternal, truly one—is dangerous, and is monotheistic/globalist in its claims. However, as we have seen with other tropes in Christian thought, Christian community undoes itself in this regard *in the midst* of its attempts at uniformity. What we long for, in short, is what will kill us. What we need is not uniformity, oneness, and fraternity. Rather, what we need is a "community of *others.*"[7]

If "the true consciousness of the loss of community is Christian," it is also true that nevertheless and in spite of all forces working against it, sometimes, indeed, community *happens*—and it can happen in the "generous abandonment" of a group of people who haltingly and with much fear and trembling call themselves Christian.[8] A community founded not on sameness, but on difference; not with the goal of a monstrous "We," but with no goal at all; a community that "present[s] . . . to its members of their mortal truth," their inevitable deaths, their "finitue and . . . irredeemable excess," is the only community that is *mitsein*, being-with. It is space itself, rather than a closed circle. It is open, as the body of Christ is opened, cut open, dead, and multiplied in the communion host and in each little gathering place. This kind of community has no goal or object; it says nothing, it does nothing. But it *shares* the space of being-in-common, the fact that "there is no singular being without another singular being."[9] In the body of Christ, as the body of Christ, the possibility of the unworking of community exists. In the end, then, the deconstruction of Christianity does not set up an either/or, a dichotomous decision to either abandon theology or subvert its language toward more secular ends. In the end, deconstructing the bodies of Christ helps us envision the space, devoid of all Western gods, where we can be, together.

NOTES

1. Leonard Cohen, "Suzanne," in *Songs of Leonard Cohen,* Sony/ATV Music Publishing LLO, 1967, renewed 1995.
2. See endnote 9 in "Introduction."
3. Nancy, *The Inoperative Community,* 141.
4. Ibid, 4.
5. Ibid.
6. Ibid, 6.
7. Ibid., 15.
8. Ibid., 10.
9. Ibid., 28.

Bibliography

Abba Isaac. "Second Conference." *The Conferences of John Cassian*. Edited by Edgar C. S. Gibson. Accessed November 2, 2016. http://www.osb.org/lectio/cassian/conf/.
Alsup, John E. *The Post-Resurrection Appearance Stories of the Gospel Tradition*. Eugene, OR: Wipf and Stock, 2007.
Alvis, Jason. "Holy Phenomenology: Heidegger's 'Phenomenology of the Inapparent' in Jean-Luc Nancy's *Adoration: The Deconstruction of Christianity II.*'" *Literature and Theology* vol. 29, no. 4 (2015): 431–449.
Athanasius. *The Letter of Athanasius to Marcinellis*. Athanasius.com. Accessed November 11, 2016. http://www.athanasius.com/psalms/aletterm.htm.
———. *On the Incarnation*. Translated by John Behr. Yonkers, NY: St. Vladimir's Seminary Press, 2012.
Augustine. "Sermon on Easter." *Catholicism.org*. Accessed October 14, 2016. http://catholicism.org/st-augustine-easter.html.
———. "Tractate CXXL." *New Advent*. Accessed September 1, 2016. http://www.newadvent.org/fathers/1701121.htm.
———. "Sermon 93." *New Advent*. Accessed September 1, 2016. http://www.newadvent.org/fathers/160393.htm.
Avis, Paul. *The Resurrection of Jesus Christ*. London, UK: Darton, Longman, and Todd, 1993.
Barth, Karl. *Church Dogmatics IV, Volume 1*. Translated by G. W. Bromiley. Edited by G. W. Bromiley and T. F. Torrance. Edinburgh, UK: T & T Clark, 1957.
Barth, Karl. "Threatened by Resurrection." *Bruderhof Communities*. Accessed November 1, 2016. http://web.archive.org/web/20030811093218/http://www.bruderhof.com/articles/Threatened.htm.
Bieler, Andrea and Luise Schottroff. *The Eucharist: Bodies, Bread, and Resurrection*. Minneapolis: Fortress Press, 2007.
Blanchot, Maurice. *Thomas the Obscure*. Translated by Robert Lamberton. Barrytown, NY: Station Hill Press, 1988.
Budge, E.A. Wallis. *The Paradise of the Holy Fathers*. Seattle: St Nectarios Press, 1984.
Bultmann, Rudolf. *New Testament and Mythology and Other Basic Writings*. Edited by Schubert M. Ogden. Philadelphia: Fortress, 1984.
Butler, Judith. *Bodies That Matter*. New York: Routledge Press, 1993.
Bynum, Caroline. *On the Resurrection of the Body in Western Christianity, 200–1336*. New York, NY: Columbia University Press, 1995.
Chrysostom, John. "Homilies on Corinthians 8, 1[2]; 24, 2[3]; 24, 2[4]; 24, 4[7]." *The Faith of the Early Fathers, Volume 2*. Translated and edited by William A. Jurgens. Collegeville, MN: The Liturgical Press, 1979.

———. "Homilies on the Gospel of John, Homily 86." *New Advent.* Accessed August 26, 2016. http://www.newadvent.org/fathers/2401.htm.

———. "Homilies on the Gospel of St. Matthew, 12." *New Advent.* Accessed November 2, 2016. http://www.newadvent.org/fathers/200112.htm.

———. "Lowliness of Mind." *New Advent.* Accessed November 2, 2016. http://www.newadvent.org/fathers/1907.htm.

Coakley, Sarah. *Religion and the Body.* Cambridge, UK: Cambridge University Press, 1997.

Collins, Ashok. "Toward a Saturated Faith: Jean-Luc Marion and Jean-Luc Nancy on the Possibility of Belief After Deconstruction." *Sophia* vol. 54 (2015): 321–341.

Cavanaugh, William T. *Torture and Eucharist.* Malden, MA: Wiley-Blackwell Publishing, 1998.

Cloots, Andre. "Christianity, Incarnation, and Disenchantment," *Radical Secularization?* Edited by Stijn Latre, Walter Van Herck, and Guido Vanheeswijck. New York: Bloomsbury Publishing, 2015.

Cyril of Alexandria. "On the Incarnation of the Only-Begotten." *Tertullian.org.* Accessed January 10, 2015. http://www.tertullian.org/fathers/cyril_scholia_incarnation_01_text.htm.

———. "Commentary on the Gospel of John 1:14." *Tertullian.org.* Accessed January 11, 2015. http://www.tertullian.org/fathers/index.htm#Cyril_Commentary_on_the_Gospel_of_John

Cyril of Jerusalem. "Catechetical Lectures, 22, 23." *New Advent.* Accessed November 2, 2016. http://www.newadvent.org/fathers/310122.htm.

———. "Homily 22." *New Advent.* Accessed November 1, 2016. http://www.newadvent.org/fathers/310122.htm.

DiNovo, Cheri. *Que(e)rying Evangelism: Growing a Community from the Outside In.* Cleveland, OH: The Pilgrim Press, 2005.

Eaghll, Tenzan. "Jean-Luc Nancy on Sovereignty and the Retreat of the Christian God." *Res Publica. Revista de Historia de las Ideas Políticas*, Vol. 17 Núm. 2 (2014): 421–434.

Eitel, Adam. "The Resurrection of Jesus Christ: Karl Barth and the Historicization of God's Being." *International Journal of Systematic Theology* vol. 10, no. 1 (2008): 36–53.

Fritz, Peter Joseph. "Capitalism—or Christianity: Creation and Incarnation in Jean-Luc Nancy." *Political Theology* 15:5 (2014), 421–437.

———. "On the V(i)erge: Jean-Luc Nancy, Christianity, and Incompletion." *The Heythrop Journal* (2014), 620–634.

Gauchet, Marcel. *The Disenchantment of the World: A Political History of Religion*, translated by Oscar Burge. Princeton, NJ: Princeton University Press, 1997.

Gorski, Philip S. and Ates Altınordu. "After Secularization?" *Annual Review of Sociology* no. 34 (2008).

Gregory the Nazanian. "The Wonder of the Incarnation." *Crossroads Initiative.* Accessed January 10, 2015. https://www.crossroadsinitiative.com/library_article/84/Wonder_of_the_Incarnation___St._Gregory_Nazianzen.htm.

Hall, Christopher A. *Worshiping with the Early Church Fathers.* Downers Grove, IL: IVP Academic, 2010.

Hemming, Laurence Paul. "The Subject of Prayer." *Blackwell Companion to Postmodern Theology.* Edited by Graham Ward. Massachusetts: Blackwell Publishers, 2001.

Heine, Ronald E. *Classical Christian Doctrine.* Grand Rapids, MI: Baker Academic Press, 2013.

Hutchens, B. C. *Jean-Luc Nancy and the Future of Philosophy.* Montreal, Quebec: McGill Queens University Press, 2005.

Ignatius. "Epistle to the Smyrnaeans." *Patristics.* Accessed November 3, 2016. http://www.patristics.co/2016/02/21/ignatius-epistle-to-the-smyrnaeans/.

———. "Letter to the Ephesians." *New Advent.* Accessed November 2, 2016. http://www.newadvent.org/cathen/12345b.htm.

———. "Letter to Romans 7:3." *New Advent.* Accessed November 1, 2016. http://www.newadvent.org/fathers/0107.htm.

Irenaeus. "Against Heresies 5:2:2–3." *New Advent.* Accessed November 1, 2016. http://www.newadvent.org/fathers/0103.htm.

James, Ian. *The Fragmentary Demand: An Introduction to the Philosophy of Jean-Luc Nancy.* Redwood City, CA: Stanford University Press, 2005.
John of Damascus. "Exposition of the Orthodox Faith." *Nicene and Post-Nicene Fathers, Second Series,* Vol. 9. Translated by E.W. Watson and L. Pullan. Edited by Philip Schaff and Henry Wace. Buffalo, NY: Christian Literature Publishing Co., 1899.
Justin the Martyr. "On the Resurrection." *New Advent.* Accessed October 3, 2016. http://www.newadvent.org/fathers/0131.htm.
Keen, Craig. *After Crucifixion.* Eugene, OR: Cascade Press, 2013.
———. *The Transgression of the Integrity of God.* Eugene, OR: Cascade Press, 2012.
Kerr, Nathan R. *Christ, History, and Apocalyptic: The Politics of Christian Mission.* Eugene, OR: Cascade Press, 2009.
Kotansky, Roy D. "The Resurrection of Jesus in Biblical Theology: From Early Appearances (1 Corinthians 15) to the 'Sindonology' of the Empty Tomb." *Reconsidering the Relationship between Biblical and Systematic Theology in the New Testament.* Edited by Benjamin E. Reynolds, Brian Lugioyo, and Kevin J. Vanhoozer. Tubingen, Germany: Mohr Siebeck, 2014.
Macquarrie, John. "The Pre-existence of Christ." *Expository Times,* vol. 77 (1966), 199–202.
Mead, G. R. S. *Fragments of a Faith Forgotten: Some Short Sketches Among the Gnostics.* Whitefish, MT: Kessinger Publishing, 2005.
Monod, Jean-Claude, "Heaven on Earth? The Löwith-Blumenberg Debate." *Radical Secularization?* Edited by Stijn Latre, Walter Van Herck, and Guido Vanheeswijck. New York: Bloomsbury Publishing, 2015.
Nancy, Jean-Luc. *Adoration: Deconstruction of Christianity II.* Translated by John McKeane. New York: Fordham University Press, 2012.
———. *Corpus.* Translated by Richard A. Rand. New York: Fordham University Press, 2008.
———. *Dis-Enclosure: The Deconstruction of Christianity.* Translated by Bettina Bergo, Gabriel Malenfant, and Michael B. Smith. New York: Fordham University Press, 2008.
———. *The Inoperative Community.* Edited by Peter Connor. Translated by Peter Connor, Lisa Garbus, Michael Holland, and Simona Sawhney. Minneapolis, MN: University of Minnesota Press, 1991.
———. *Noli Me Tangere: On the Raising of the Body.* Translated by Sarah Clift, Pascale-Anne Brault, and Michael Nass. New York: Fordham University Press, 2008.
Origen. "Gospel of John, Book II." *New Advent.* Accessed October 5, 2016. http://www.newadvent.org/fathers/101502.htm.
Pannenberg, Wolfhardt. *Jesus: God and Man.* Translated by Lewis L. Wilkins and Duane A. Priebe. Philadelphia, PA: The Westminster Press, 1977.
Parmenides. "Fr. 8, 22–5, Simplicius in Phys. 144, 29." *The Pre-Socratic Philosophers.* Edited by G. S. Kirk, J. E. Raven, and M. Schofield. Cambridge, UK: Cambridge University Press, 1983.
Robinette, Brian. *Grammars of Resurrection: A Christian Theology of Presence and Absence.* Spring Valley, NY: The Crossroad Publishing Co., 2009.
Ross, Susan A. *Extravagant Affections: A Feminist Sacramental Theology.* New York: Continuum Publishing Company, 1998.
Rugo, Daniele. *Jean-Luc Nancy and the Thinking of Otherness.* New York: Bloomsbury Academic Press, 2013.
Saghafi, Kas. "Thomas the Marvelous: Resurrection and Living-Death in Blanchot and Nancy." *Mosaic* vol. 45, no. 3 (2012), 1–16.
Schaef, Philip. "Creeds of Christendom, with a History and Critical Notes, Vol. 2." *Christian Classics Ethereal Library.* Accessed January 11, 2015. http://www.ccel.org/ccel/schaff/creeds2.
Ward, Benedicta and Anthony Bloom. *Wisdom of the Desert Fathers.* Collegeville, MN: Cistercian Publications, 2006.
Watkin, Christopher. *Difficult Atheism: Post-Theological Thinking in Alain Badiou, Jean-Luc Nancy, and Quentin Meillassoux.* Edinburgh: Edinburgh University Press, 2011.
Wayman, Benjamin. *Make the Words Your Own: An Early Christian Guide to the Psalms.* Brewster, MA: Paraclete Press, 2014.

Index

Abba Isaac, xviiin21, 72, 73
Absence/absenting, x–xi, 28, 37, 39, 42–44, 48, 50, 50–51, 59, 62, 72, 74, 75, 77, 78, 79–80, 81, 84, 92
Adoration, x, xvi, 9, 58, 59–60, 62, 64, 67, 69–74, 76, 77, 79, 83, 85, 91
Adorno, Theodore, 70
Alvis, Jason, 44
Anselm, 45
Aquinas, 12, 34, 63
Athanasius, 14, 73
Augustine, 29, 31, 41, 42

Badiou, Alain, 21
Barth, Karl, xv, 36, 37, 45–47
Being-with, x, 49, 50, 53, 58, 69, 70, 77–78, 83, 84, 86, 91, 92, 94
Bieler, Andrea, xv, 47, 48, 64
Blanchot, Maurice, 32, 35, 38, 38–39, 44, 51
Blumenberg, Hans, x
Body/bodies, xiii, xiv, 2, 3, 4, 5, 6, 9, 9–10, 11, 15, 16, 17–18, 18, 21–22, 32, 36, 40, 43, 44, 48, 49–50, 58, 61, 62, 63, 64, 65, 67, 68, 73, 75–81, 91, 92; Of Christ, xi–xii, xiv, 10, 36, 37, 41, 43, 48, 57, 58, 65, 66, 84, 92, 94
Buber, Martin, 47, 77
Bultmann, Rudolph, 45
Bynum, Caroline, 32, 36

Cavanaugh, William T., xv, 58, 67–69
Church. *See* ecclesia.
Celsus, 35
Chrysostom, 25n51, 42, 62, 63, 72
Cloots, Andre, xviiin24
Coakley, Sarah, 24n44, 33
Cohen, Leonard, 92
Collins, Ashok, 43, 50
Community, ix, 57, 58
Corpus. *See* bodies.
Creation, x, 6, 8, 12, 15, 17, 32, 36, 37, 46–47, 48–49, 52, 65, 92
Cyril of Alexandria, xviiin14, 12
Cyril of Jerusalem, 60, 62

Dawkins, Christopher, 88n55
Dead/death, x, xi, xiii, xv, 9, 11, 13, 14, 27–30, 31, 34, 35–37, 37, 38–39, 41, 44, 47, 50, 51, 52, 52–53, 60, 62, 64–65, 70, 75, 83, 84, 85, 92, 94
Deconstruction of Christianity, ix, xi, xiii, xiii–xiv, xvi, 1, 3, 9, 21–22, 30, 35, 38, 40, 53, 57, 58, 60, 63, 64, 66, 69–70, 72, 79, 81, 82, 83–84, 85, 86, 91, 92, 93, 94
Derrida, Jacques, ix, xiv, 50, 79, 80, 82
Desert Fathers, xv, 72, 73, 81
DiNovo, Cheri, xiv, xvi, 3, 52–53, 75, 82–84
Doctrine, xi, xiii–xiv, xv, xvi, 1–3, 3–4, 6, 9, 13, 15, 17, 20, 21–22, 27, 33–34, 35,

37, 39, 40, 46, 49, 65, 69, 81, 92–93

Eaghill, Tenzan, 38
Ecclesia, xvi, 57–58, 58, 59, 68–69, 73, 78, 85–86, 92
Economics, 64, 65, 83
Eitel, Adam, 46
Eucharist, xv–xvi, 6, 32, 47–48, 57, 58, 59–69, 63, 73, 75, 85–86

Faith, xi, xiii–xiv, xv–xvi, 1, 8, 9, 21, 29, 30, 31, 37, 40, 42, 43, 45, 47, 50–51, 53, 57–58, 59–60, 62, 63, 64, 65, 68, 69, 73, 74, 78–86, 93
Flesh, xi, 4, 7–8, 9, 9–10, 11–12, 14, 15, 16, 19, 21, 22, 28, 29, 31–33, 36, 38, 41, 44, 51, 61–62, 66, 69, 81, 83, 91. *See also* bodies
Foucault, Michel, 83
Fritz, Peter Joseph, xviiin21

Gauchet, Marcel, x
Gnostics, 29, 61, 65
Granel, Gerard, 80
Gregory of Nazianzus, 11
Gregory of Nyssa, 48, 49, 60, 72
Gschwandtner, Christina, 56n106

Hall, Christopher A., 74, 86n10
Heidegger, Martin, ix, 49, 76, 77, 80
Heine, Ronald, 23n4
Heming, Lawrence Paul, xv, 76–78, 85
Hutchens, BC, 3

Ignatius, 61, 73, 81
Incarnation, xiv, 1–5, 6–8, 9–11, 13, 14–15, 16–18, 19–20, 21–22, 27, 29, 30, 35, 35–36, 37, 51, 52, 57, 59, 60, 65, 69, 71, 85, 92
Irenaeus, xiii, 29, 32, 44, 61

James, Ian, xi
Janicaud, Dominique, xiii
John of Damascus, 81–82
John Scotus, 33
Justin Martyr, 25n51, 42

Kant, Immanuel, 45

Keen, Craig, xiv–62, 3, 18–19, 52–53, 58, 66–67, 75–76, 84–85
Kenosis/kenotic, xiv, 3, 8, 10–11, 16–18, 22, 52, 75
Kerr, Nathan, 85
Kierkegaard, Soren, 16, 85, 94
Kotansky, Roy D., 55n57

Lachterman, David, 76
Lambert, Gregg, xiv
Leder, Drew, 51, 52
Levinas, Emmanuel, 71, 76, 82
Löwith, Karl, x

Macquarrie, John, 3, 17
Marion, Jean-Luc, 48, 50, 68, 76, 78
Merleau-Ponty, Maurice, 54n32
Monod, Jean-Claude, x
Monotheism, x, x–xi, xviin10, 1, 3, 6, 9, 15, 47, 52, 70, 92, 94

Nestorius, xviiin14, 12
Nietzsche, Friedrich, ix, 77, 81

Ontology, ix, x, xi, xiii, xiv, 3, 5, 9, 15, 17, 19, 21, 70, 76, 77, 80; Relational, 6–7, 9, 10, 17–18, 21, 65, 68, 69, 70, 71, 83
Onto-theology, xiv, xvi, 12, 18, 19, 40, 45, 46, 50–51, 52, 77, 80, 81, 84, 86
Open/openness, xi–xii, xiii, xiv, 1–3, 4, 5–7, 8, 9–10, 13, 15, 19, 21, 22, 35, 37, 44, 48, 52, 63, 69–70, 71, 73–74, 75, 76, 77, 80, 81, 84, 85, 94
Origen, 16, 31, 41

Pannenberg, Wolfhardt, 23n4
Phenomenology, 48–51
Politics/political, ix, ix–x, x, xv, 20, 48, 64–65, 66, 67, 78, 82, 85, 93, 93–94
Prayer, xv, 9, 58, 60, 63, 66, 69–70, 72–77, 79, 80, 83, 85, 85–86

Queer, xiv, 3, 20–21, 82–83, 93

Raffoul, François, xviiin22
Ratzinger, Karl, 60
Resurrection, xv, xvi, 4, 19, 27–29, 30, 32–34, 35, 36, 36–37, 38, 40, 41, 43, 44, 84; Of Christ, ix, xi, xiv, xv, 19, 28,

29, 29–31, 34, 36, 37, 39, 41–42, 45, 46–47, 47–53, 57, 60, 64, 65, 75, 84, 85, 92
Robinette, Brian, xv, 45, 48–51
Ross, Susan A., xv, 65
Rueffer, Rosemary Radford, 66
Rugo, Daniele, xi, 3

Saghafi, Kas, 55n43
Samuelson, Norbert, 24n41
Schottroff, Luise, xv–xvi, 47–48, 64
Schmemman, Alexander, 84
Sense, xii, xv, 1, 3, 5, 6, 21, 23n17, 27, 35–36, 37, 37–38, 39, 43, 50, 51, 70, 71, 77, 92
Space, x, xii, xiv, 4, 6, 7, 11, 18, 22, 37, 39, 43, 57, 59, 64, 68–69, 70, 73, 76, 78, 81, 83, 84, 85, 92, 94

Taylor, Mark Lewis, xviiin20, 19
Tertullian, xviiin14, 12, 60
Tillich, Paul, 17

Watkin, Christopher, xviiin22
Wayman, Benjamin, 73
Wesley, John, 84

About the Author

Christina Smerick is Professor of Philosophy, Chair of the Bastian School of Theology, Philosophy, and Ministry, and Dean of Instruction at Greenville University in Greenville, Illinois. She received her Ph.D. in Philosophy from DePaul University. Her recent publications include "No Other Place to Be: Globalization, Monotheism, and *Salut* in Jean-Luc Nancy," in *Thinking Plural: Expositions of Jean-Luc Nancy on World, Art, and Meaning* with SUNY Press; and "Bodies, Communities, Faith: Christian Legacies in Jean-Luc Nancy," in *Analecta Hermeneutica.* No. 4 (2012). Her edited volume, *"This Is My Body": Embodiment in a Wesleyan Spirit,* is with Pickwick Press.

www.ingramcontent.com/pod-product-compliance
Lightning Source LLC
Chambersburg PA
CBHW022016300426
44117CB00005B/213